Armenien MAIOR

Beleania

r1 Soltanea Das Grosse

Anzeta AR MENIA

Niphats Geburg Das Geburg Niphats

Calacine

Segira

Arsamesata Marde Calah Oroba

Derheta Gemara Arbe Iutis

Taurus Geburg ASSUR Sura

Saccana nun genant Das Geburg Ararat

Suma Nisibis Deba Adiabene darauf die Arch Noe

Porsica Hiddekel Arbela Appolonia ruhet Gen 8.4

Edessa Singara Ac cad Resen Arthemita Thebura

Ombrea Das Geburg Meschia ASSYRIEN. Cinna

Zeugma MESO Zama Ninive Thelbe

Phrath fluu Balatha SO Betum Calne Sitace

Haran ARAM Geburg von Osten Ur

PADDAN Schwer Vatter flohe Ex 3l Dabusa CHAL DEA Sephar Hiddekel Closiphon

Acraba Elia Peliala Diamatra Babel DEN Sacron

Zura PO Chabora Phrath fluu Paradys NO

Maube TAMIA Pethor Gihon E

Alalis Darema von hier auwird Volgesta

Alamatha Tipsacus Euphrates Bileam geholet Bela I Agra Melitena

Irsa Thelda Bethauna Israel zu fluchen N Cumana

Adada Zita Num 22 v5 Punda HA

dea Dadara Addea Idiaera B Arac

Pal Dedan Balagala Eutrapa Cesa Orchoa I Tartana A

mi Cathany Colarina Belginea L Talatha VI

rena Scheba Sabe Cauchabem Biaramba O R

Averia Kadar. Regania Telme N Aschia LA

Choe DAS LAND Iamba I Tigris Graam

accea Alata Thema Sortida A Teredon Passinivallum Peloa

hea Agreni Thema Duma E Balsera

reisch CUS nun genant Duma N Das Cap

oth wüest. Macani .

TEN Thauba Seraa Naphis Cera LIT Kedmais SIN

ARA E BIEN. Calathua Idiaera

Aguberii Banacha ISMA Bere Salma Itara

Arthemita Dumetha Rhabani Orcheni

Das Arabische Geburg

Diese Landt Charte soll ge
hefftet werden vor das
3 Cap Genesis

IN THE
FOOTSTEPS
OF THE PROPHETS

IN THE FOOTSTEPS OF THE PROPHETS

LEON AMIEL
PUBLISHER

MOSHE PEARLMAN

PHOTOGRAPHY BY DAVID HARRIS

GENERAL EDITOR MORDECAI RAANAN
DESIGN CONSULTANT GAD ULMAN

First Printing, January 1975
Second Printing, July 1976
Third Printing, July 1977
Fourth Printing, April 1978

Published in:
Israel, by Nateev Publishing House, Tel-Aviv
United States of America, by Leon Amiel Publisher, New York
Switzerland, by Walter Verlag, Olten und Freiburg im Breisgau
France, by Editions Arthaud, Paris et Grenoble
Holland, by Amsterdam Boek, Amsterdam
Sweden, by Harriers Bokforlag AB, Stockholm
Japan, by Kodansha, Tokio
South Africa, by NG Kerkboekhandel, Pretoria

ACKNOWLEDGMENTS and thanks are due to the following institutions and persons for having kindly permitted their exhibits to be photographed:
Department of Antiquities and Museums, Ministry of Education and Culture, Jerusalem, pages 29, 32, 35, 46, 47, 59, 63, 82, 91, 99, 115, 134, 137, 148, 165,
182, 190, 191, 211; The Library of St. Thoros, The Armenian Patriarchate, Jerusalem, page 73; The National Maritime Museum, Haifa, page 79; The
Westminster Press, Philadelphia, Pa., pages 92, 196; Princeton University Press, New-Jersy, page 94; Israel Museum, Jerusalem, page 109; The Shrine of the
Book, Israel Museum, Jerusalem, pages 111, 194; British Museum, London, pages 124, 145, 200; The Jewish National and University Library, Jerusalem,
page 176. Photograph by Studio Garo, Jerusalem, page 216.

Printed in Israel, by Peli Printing Works Ltd.

CONTENTS

AUTHOR'S NOTE

This book is a companion volume to my IN THE FOOTSTEPS OF MOSES, and takes up the story
of the ancient Hebrews where the other left off. The period it covers begins with Samuel in the
latter half of the 11th century BC and ends with "the last of the prophets" in the 6th century BC.
It is concerned primarily with the part played by the prophets in nurturing the Jewish religion
and the Jewish nation in their formative years.
However, I have thought it well to provide two brief introductory chapters on Moses, Joshua and
the Judges, the central figures who helped lay the foundations of the faith and the nation from
the 13th to the 11th centuries BC. For this, I have drawn on material in IN THE FOOTSTEPS
OF MOSES, with the kind permission of the publishers, and I thank them.
I also thank Dr. Moshe Weinfeld, Professor of Biblical Studies at the Hebrew University
of Jerusalem, who read the manuscript and made very valuable suggestions; Dr. Magen Broshi,
Curator of the Shrine of the Book, Israel Museum, Jerusalem, and Ze'ev Yeivin, of the Israel
Government's Department of Antiquities, who helped in the selection of the illustrations;
and Judith Lelyveld, who also helped with the illustrations and applied meticulous care in
seeing the book through the press.

Jerusalem, June 1975.   Moshe Pearlman

Some were fiery, impulsive, primitive, eccentric; others were thoughtful, soft-spoken, conventional, sophisticated. One fled for his life from the wrath of a queen; another was courted by kings. Some walked with ease through the corridors of power; others were at home only in a peasant's tent. Some were farmers or herdsmen, musing on the profundities of human existence while tilling the soil or wandering with their flocks. Others were scholars, masters of statecraft, whose counsel was sought, or suffered, by the royal chancelleries.

Yet different as they were, the one from the other, in background, personality and style, all were seized with a burning passion to root out wickedness and draw forth the righteousness in man. All were powerful fighters for justice, fearless and outspoken, denouncing venality at a time when death was often the penalty for frankness. All, indeed, had courage; and they also had compassion. All were visionaries, fountains of inspired truth, revered (though not always by the targets of their tongues) as divine spokesmen who bore the word of God to the people. They were well equipped for this task, for all were touched by the magic of poetic genius, with an unmatched gift for language and imagery, and their sublime words had an overpowering and unprecedented impact on human behavior ever after.

These men were the Hebrew prophets of old, whose nobility of thought and grandeur of expression are as moving and as relevant today as they were when first given voice some 3,000 years ago.

Each prophet had his own idiom and each spoke in the context of his times; but the theme common to all — in a tempting world of easy paganism — was Israelite monotheism and the enlightened code of behavior which the people of Israel accepted in a binding Covenant with God at Mount Sinai. In the generations subsequent to that dramatic 13th century BC Covenant ceremony, conducted through Moses, the prophets sought to stir the conscience of the nation, using their imaginative talents to remind it of its contractual obligations.

Not always, indeed not often, were they successful in their immediate purpose. But their success, which was to prove more lasting, lay in conditioning the nation to the Mosaic Covenant tradition. Thus it was that, centuries later, established in their Promised Land, the people were still receptive to an appeal to the spirit and uncommonly endowed with a reverence for the word, their ears and hearts attuned to a lofty thought and an illustrious phrase. Even when they failed at the time to heed what they heard, they at least delighted in the exhortations of their poet-prophets. They savoured them, relished them and repeated them, and — usually when catastrophe followed non-compliance — remembered them, and handed them on from generation to generation.

In the case of those who are known as the "Former Prophets", only much later were their words committed to writing. These men, who lived between the 13th and 9th centuries BC, are often called the popular or pre-classical prophets, and their utterances and deeds have come down to us in the accounts of their lives which appear in the biblical Books of Joshua, Judges, Samuel and Kings. Those known as the "Later Prophets" (covering the period from the 8th to the 5th century BC), whom scholars call the classical or literary prophets, are those whose words were often written down at the time, either by themselves or their scribes or disciples, and are preserved in the biblical Books of Isaiah, Jeremiah and Ezekiel, and in the Books of the Twelve who are known as the Minor Prophets (the term relates not necessarily to the measure of their importance but to the volume of their writings): Hosea, Joel, Amos, Obadiah, Jonah, Micah, Nahum, Habakkuk, Zephaniah, Haggai, Zechariah and Malachi.

Through the preservation of these prophetic utterances, first orally and later in script, the Jewish people already in the 1st millennium BC treasured and held sacred a body of writing, in exquisite Hebrew style, which set forth a profound and enlightened system of relationships of man to man and man to God which was eventually to form the basis of western civilization.

These ethical and religious writings, together with the Law (the Torah) and the chronicles of the deeds of their forebears, held the collective memory and the collective wisdom of the Jewish nation. ("The Books", as they were called ["Ha-Sefarim" in Hebrew, "Biblia" in Greek], would much later be formally canonized as the Bible.) Venerated, read and studied by every successive Jewish generation, they contained the supreme code of Jewish life, gave the Jews their specific religion and identity, and preserved them as a people, nourishing their hopes at all times, sobering them in their triumphs, encouraging them in their trials, guiding and sustaining them throughout all the centuries of their vicissitudes.

The prophets spoke to a specific people at a specific time. The impact of their words was to be universal and timeless.

1. THE FIRST AND THE GREATEST

As torch bearers of the Covenant tradition, most vocal when the thread leading back to Sinai seemed most fragile, the prophets led lonely, dangerous and challenging lives. But none faced such gigantic challenges as those tackled by Moses, first and greatest of the prophets, and the man who had started the tradition.

He was of course very much more than a prophet, and his tasks and his genius were more wide-ranging than those of his spiritual successors. He was the founder of the Jewish faith, the mediator of God's Covenant with his people, the instrument through which they were given a unique code of religious and ethical principles. But his contribution in the secular sphere was equally fundamental, for he was also the founder of the Jewish nation — resistance leader, liberator, statesman, military commander, and supreme moral and political guide. His spiritual inspiration was the key to his secular success; and it was his secular power which made possible the attainment of his spiritual purpose in his lifetime — an accomplishment often denied the prophets who followed him.

Moses was born in Egypt at a time when the Israelites were state-slaves suffering cruel oppression. The reigning pharaoh, Sethos I (1309–1290 BC), had decreed that all Hebrew male infants were to be drowned at birth in the Nile; but Moses was rescued by the monarch's daughter, taken to the royal palace and brought up as a prince. It was no doubt at the very court of this all-powerful Sethos that he acquired an understanding of political, military and administrative affairs which — without knowing it at the time — would stand him in crucial stead in later years. Whenever the opportunity offered, he must have followed with the keenest interest the conduct of state business, the process of decision-making and the patterns of diplomacy and warfare. From royal counsellors, court chamberlains and public officials, he would have picked up much valuable information on the management of people. Army commanders and executives in charge of slave projects who came to the palace to report to the pharaoh would have been pleased to satisfy the young prince's curiosity about logistics and the organization and movement of large

Temple to the Egyptian goddess Hathor
at Serabit el-Khadem, established for
the Egyptian overseers of the Semitic slaves
who worked in the quarries.

formations; and if not they, their aides, whom Moses would encounter in the royal ante-chambers.

Yet while living the life of a prince, he had evidently been made secretly aware of his origins — probably through his sister Miriam, at clandestine meetings arranged by his foster-mother. From her anguished reports on the treatment of slaves — a subject dismissed with derision in the talk at court — he would have known of the grim trials being suffered by his people. This must have roused in him a sense of justice rare at the time, and fired his resolution to right the grievous wrong.

One of his first acts on reaching manhood was to visit a forced-labour project, where he saw an Egyptian overseer maltreating a Hebrew slave. This so incensed him that he promptly killed the Egyptian. It was a capital offence to strike, let alone kill, a task-master — for this endangered the entire slave system of Egypt — and Moses fled to the desert. There he was given hospitality by Jethro, a Midianite priest, whose daughter he eventually married. He spent the next few years wandering across the expanse of the Sinai wilder-

11

It was from quarries like this
that the huge stones were
extracted by slave labour and used
for the construction of the pyramids.

ness with his father-in-law's flocks, acquiring in the process an intimate knowledge of life in the desert, an awareness of its dangers and meager blessings, a familiarity with its terrain and its moods in each season. As with his experience as a prince at court, this knowledge, too, would prove invaluable to him later.

DIVINE ASSIGNMENT

In the desert he also found enlightenment of deeper significance. As he roamed in search of scrub for his animals, his mind was equally free to roam, and he must surely have reflected on the strange events which had led to his current lot, from his miraculous rescue as a baby and his royal upringing in the very citadel of his people's oppressor, to the circumstance which had forced him to flee. At the heart of this last incident was his revulsion of slavery, of man's oppression of man, of the injustice which had forced the Hebrews into bondage.

He would have recalled the surreptitious talks with his sister Miriam about the sad condition of their people, and he would have remembered what she had told him of the invisible God who had formed a Covenant with their Patriarch Abraham. At the time, pagan priests and idol-worship had been part of his royal life, and he had found it hard to grasp the peculiar notion of an all-powerful divinity who could neither be touched nor seen. Now, however, and here in the silent, empty desert, he was alone with the elements of nature. They were powerful and mysterious, and he had begun to sense that they were controlled and directed by a guiding hand. Assuredly, such guidance could never come from the mute and man-made deities he had seen in his youth. It must come from the invisible God of which Miriam had spoken, and He must have a cosmic design and a cosmic purpose. Perhaps, then, there might be a design after all to the curious turns of fortune which had marked his own young life, and its meaning would become apparent one day.

It was presumably amidst such mediations that Moses experienced his startling encounter with the Lord, the "God of Abraham, of Isaac, and of Jacob", as a voice calling to him

Tents made of goats' hair
Throughout the centuries, the tribes
of the desert have fashioned their mobile
dwellings from materials close at hand.

from a burning bush giving him His divine assignment. The Israelites would be delivered out of the hand of the Egyptians and be brought to the Promised Land in fulfillment of God's Covenant with their Patriarchs. Moses would be the instrument of their redemption.

Suddenly, everything fell into place in Moses' mind: all that had ever happened to him since birth made sense. Each event, each experience, each episode had had its purpose, and the overall purpose had now been revealed by the divine voice from the flaming bush. His entire life so far had been a preparation for his role of destiny, and he had been given his goal — the salvation of his people. Henceforth, without hesitation, or doubt, guided by the God of his fathers, he would move unflichingly towards it.

EXODUS

By now, the capital offence committed when he was a young man was forgotten, and Moses could safely return to Egypt. His first task was to meet with his people, who were organized in clans within the twelve Hebrew tribal groups, and bring them the divine message of salvation. Together with his brother, Aaron, he held preliminary sessions with "all the elders . . . of Israel" — the clan and tribal leaders — and sought to win their confidence and rouse them to resistance with the stupendous news that their days of slavery were about to end and that freedom was a practical goal. The resistance aim was not to overthrow the existing pharaonic regime but to compel it to let its slaves depart. They would leave for their own promised land where they would be free to worship the one invisible God and develop their own national life.

Moses must have had an agonizing time trying to persuade his people to launch themselves on a course fraught with such danger, turning on their masters and taking the great leap into the unknown. There would also have been reluctance from some of the tribal chiefs to surrender part of their authority to the overall leadership of this strange man, with his unusual — though admittedly inspiring — tale of a wilderness revelation and his extraordinary visions of a wondrous future. But Moses was eventually successful in se-

The Exodus of the Israelites from Egypt was so hasty
that they had to take "their dough before it was leavened."
This is commemorated during the Jewish Festival of
Passover by the eating of **matza,** unleavened bread.
There are parts of Sinai where **matza** is still baked in
the ancient way, as shown in these photographs.
The dough (flour and water) is being kneaded,
a pit prepared and glowing charcoal placed at the bottom.
The rolled dough is spread over the charcoal, covered by
another layer of charcoal , and left to bake.

curing their trust, and he and Aaron could proceed to their difficult task of approaching the pharaoh — now the redoutable Rameses II, son of Sethos — with the brazen demand to "let my people go".

Unmoved by Moses' arguments to free the Hebrew serfs, Rameses was "persuaded" by the ten plagues to rid his country of the Israelites, and Moses led them out in their Exodus. Within days he was faced with a monumental crisis, when his people were caught between the sea and the charging chariots of the Egyptians, who had recovered their nerve and had second thoughts. The miracle of the parting of the waters followed, and the Israelites reached the western edge of the Sinai wilderness to begin their great trek to freedom.

After months of weary wandering, often "murmuring" against Moses for exposing them to hunger, thirst and the unaccustomed day and night extremes of desert temperatures, the people arrived at the foot of Mount Sinai. Bringing them this far from serfdom in Egypt was a singular feat of leadership on Moses' part. He was now to reach the spiritual peak, playing the key human role in a climatic event that was to shape the moral and physical lives of the Jewish people ever after.

THE COVENANT

Moses was the medium through which the Covenant was concluded between God and the Israelites — the detailed covenant procedure is recorded in Exodus 19 — and under its terms the people agreed to accept and be bound by the divine code, the Ten Commandments. These were landmark guidelines of human behavior, which are respected today, more than three millennia later, as the touchstone of civilized life. At that time, however, the idea of one invisible God, and the propositions that killing was abominable, theft reprehensible, worship of idols and abhorrence, the *Shabbat* a vital safeguard for the health of the working population, and respect for one's neighbor crucial to a harmonious society, were startling and revolutionary. The Decalogue marked an historic break from the prevailing views, customs and practices, and it represented a giant advance in the conception of man's relationship to man and to God.

The Covenant act and the Covenant text, the Ten Commandments, were the foundation stones of Israel's nationhood, welding together as a distinct religious and political community the twelve tribes who had recently emerged from state-slavery. Their acknowledgement of this new and binding system of laws — the Commandments were followed by a comprehensive series of religious and secular ordinances known as the Covenant Code (listed in Exodus 21–23) — was a prerequisite for unity; and Moses the statesman knew that unity was essential for the hard tasks that lay ahead. The later prophets were to know this too, and they would stress, as did Moses, the ideals of the just society and reverence for the Law both as noble ends in themselves and as the key to unity through which the nation would be preserved.

Moses faced problems far more complicated than those encountered by his prophetic successors, for he had to mould the nation in its formative years when it was still journeying towards its goal. However, he could exercise political power, whereas the sole instrument of the later prophets was their voice. They

had to persuade with words. Moses had to do that too; but when words failed, he could use his power — taking ruthless action at times (as he did over the incident of the golden calf) to secure general adherence to the Law.

"HEAR, O ISRAEL"

Of the forty years spent by the Israelites in the wilderness, there was a thirty-eight-year sojourn in Kadesh Barnea, some fifty miles south of Beersheba, and it was there that Moses prepared the younger generation both spiritually and physically for the next giant step they, and they alone, would be taking: entry into the Promised Land and their establishment as an independent nation. He underlined the supremacy of the Sinai Covenant, developed the religious code, extended the civil laws, tightened his administrative organization, guided and trained subordinates to whom he could delegate authority, and ordered military training (probably under the direction of Joshua).

The first major test of battle came when they left Kadesh on their last lap, and Moses showed military wisdom in choosing a long roundabout route to reach their goal. The short direct route would have brought his untrained men too soon up against skilled warriors and tough defences. The longer route gave them the opportunity of trying their military mettle in skirmishes and less critical battles. By the time they reached, fought their way along and occupied a broad belt of the eastern bank of the river Jordan, they were combat-hardened and ready to begin the conquest and settlement of the Promised Land.

Thanks to Moses, the new generation of Israelites could meet this challenge — and their destiny — with confidence. It was he, under divine guidance, who had rallied their parents to resistance, broken their fetters and led them safely through the desert. His function had been pivotal in the forging of God's Covenant with the people, and the establishment of a unique religion. He had moulded the various clans into an embryo nation, and laid the basis of a national discipline through the provision of a central legal structure. And it was he who had kept alive the spirit of

Part of a primitive hunting scene (right)
with camel riders and trappers on foot,
scratched on sandstone rock. Graffiti by travellers
and pilgrims of different historical
periods are to be found along the caravan
routes throughout Sinai. Among the rock
drawings found in Sinai was this representation of
a menorah , the seven-branched candelabrum
described in the vision of Zechariah (4:2) which
became the Jewish symbol of the light of
the spirit and its supremacy over might.
The menorah was one of the ritual vessels
in the Second Temple. It is today
the emblem of the State of Israel.

freedom, his eye fixed constantly on the goal of liberation, urging his people forward, at times gentle, at times drastic, tending to their physical wants and stiffening their morale in moments of despair, seeking at all times to fill their hearts with his own sense of purpose.

His task was now done, though he must have been sorely grieved at being allowed only to glimpse, but not to enter, the Promised Land. He could draw comfort from the thought that what he and the generation of bondsmen had achieved had been essential, and that, with all their shortcomings, it had been their extraordinary strivings and grim sufferings which had brought their children within reach of the fruits. He and they together had laid the foundations. It was now up to the young to meet the next crucial phase in the struggle for independence in their own land. He had confidence in them and in the man who would lead them — his successor would be Joshua — and he had no doubt that, if they remained faithful to the Lord's Covenant, they would prove equal to their task.

Before he died, Moses gave a series of

The oasis of Ein Furtaga in eastern Sinai. This is a rare photograph of a "sea in the desert", waters rushing down after heavy rains in the distant north and briefly trapped in a flash-flood in the wadi.

23

farewell addresses to the congregation of Israel (recorded in the first person in Deuteronomy), and his words were to be echoed in varied forms by the prophets who followed him. To the children and grandchildren of state-slaves who had started the great freedom march, Moses the educator recounted the drama of the Exodus and the trek through the wilderness, and exhorted them never to forget it, nor their origins. Moses the prophet and Law-giver recalled the Commandments and the Covenant Code. And Moses the national leader gave them guidance on their future behaviour when they came to settle in their land. The striking valedictory utterance which served ever after as the most solemn declaration of the faith was his "Shema Yisrael", the most noted prayer in the Hebrew Prayer Book: "Hear, O Israel: The Lord our God is one Lord . . . And these words which I command you this day shall be upon your heart; and you shall teach them diligently to your children . . ." (Deut. 6:4–7). The injunction to teach "these words . . . to your children" was faithfully followed through all the subsequent generations and centuries, and

is assuredly one of the reasons for Jewish survival.

Moses died "in a valley in the land of Moab . . . but no man knows the place of his burial to this day" (Deut. 34:6). The concealment of his sepulchre was clearly deliberate, to prevent its becoming a cultic site which might have led to his deification. "And there has not arisen a prophet since in Israel like Moses, whom the Lord knew face to face" (Deut. 34:10).

2. THE EARLY DAYS

Joshua is known largely as the warrior-leader, and his military prowess was indeed formidable. In his conduct of the long and tough campaign to subdue the myriad petty kingdoms and semi-nomadic groups in the land of Canaan, he proved himself an ingenious and magnetic commander, wise in strategy, resourceful in tactics, daring in combat. However, at no time did he forget that he was successor not only to Moses the national leader but also to Moses the prophet, and he did much to deepen the religious and ethical consciousness of the people. It is clear from his record that he considered his military command and his spiritual guidance as inseparable functions of his leadership.

He took the early opportunity — shortly after the battle of Ai, which had followed the Israelite success at Jericho — to assemble the people on the slopes of Mounts Ebal and Gerizim, and there "he wrote upon the stones a copy of the law of Moses . . . And afterward he heard all the words of the law, the blessing and the curse, according to all that is written in the book of the law. There was not a word of all that Moses commanded which Joshua did not read before all the assembly of Israel . . ." (Josh. 8:32–35). At similar gatherings between battles throughout the campaign, Joshua exhorted his followers to hold firm to the Mosaic Covenant and to "take good care to observe the commandment and the law . . . to love the Lord your God, and to walk in all his ways . . ." (Josh. 22:5).

JOSHUA THE CONQUEROR

His appeal to the spirit undoubtedly had a bracing effect on the morale of his fighting troops and a corresponding impact on the course of the war. He and his men faced no light campaign. They had to overcome defensive obstacles — considerable by their standards — to achieve victory. These obstacles were rarely intended to stop the war machines of mighty empires from north and south which periodically ravaged Canaan as they clashed with each other on its soil. In such encounters, the local peoples remained for the most part neutral and submitted to the tutelage of the victor. Their defences were designed primarily to frustrate attack by a close neighbor or a non-sophisticated invasion by a semi-nomadic group, like the Israelites, and they often proved highly effective.

They had every reason to believe that they would prove adequate against Joshua. The Israelites were poorly armed (at the beginning), and lacked the standard military resources of the period. Possessing no means to scale, undermine or breach the ramparts of a walled city, Joshua had to resort to stratagem, as he did at Jericho and Ai, and rely on the superior fighting spirit of his troops. High morale was equally important in the tough conventional fighting in open terrain, which was a feature of many later battles. With each success, the Israelites became stronger, more confident, more skilful and more seasoned. Their growing reputation also served to weaken the ardor or their potential enemies, and several sought hasty pacts with Joshua to avoid an armed clash.

By the end of the campaign, the Israelites were in control of most of the country, and Joshua gathered "the whole congregation of the children of Israel" at Shiloh, some twenty miles north of Jerusalem, and there he "set up the tent of meeting" (Josh. 18:1). Shiloh was probably the first site of Jewish religious pilgrimage when the tribes were settled, in accordance with the injunction in Exodus 23:17 and 34:23 and in Deuteronomy 16:16): "Three times a year all your males shall appear before the Lord God at the place which He will choose: at the feast of unleavened bread [Pesah, or Passover], at the feast of weeks [Shavuot, or Pentecost], and at the feast of booths [Succoth]." (During almost the next two centuries, the Ark of the Law [or the Ark of the Covenant] would be moved from one tribal centre to another, so that it remained for a period with each tribe. Its last temporary site was again Shiloh, towards the end of the 11th century BC. At the beginning of the 10th century, David brought the Ark to Jerusalem, and thereafter Jerusalem became its permanent home and the permanent centre of Jewish pilgrimage.)

With the fighting over, the tribes could start the settlement of their designated areas. Five of the tribes were allotted specific regions. The rest of the land was divided by lot among the remaining seven. The lots were drawn at a special assembly which Joshua

It was across the easily passable
fords of the narrow river Jordan
that the Israelites entered Canaan.

29

convened at Shiloh. Included in the distribution for future settlement were those areas which had not yet been subdued, for it is evident from the Books of Joshua and Judges that while Joshua succeeded in conquering almost the entire country, the extreme north of Canaan and the coastal plain remained unvanquished at his death. There were also several strongholds in the centre, like the cities of Jerusalem and Gezer, which were to continue for a time as enemy enclaves within Israel.

Before he died, Joshua "gathered all the tribes of Israel to Shechem", and there, at a solemn assembly, he "made a covenant with the people that day, and made statutes and ordinances for them ... And Joshua wrote these words in the book of the law of God" (Josh. 24:1, 25[26]). This ceremony was a renewal of the Sinai Covenant, and it was held in Shechem probably to dramatize the greatest danger to the Covenant tradition — the influence of paganism. (The local Shechemites maintained friendly relations with the Israelites, but they were pagans, and Joshua no doubt chose this location as an example to warn the tribes against the possibly contagious rites of their neighbors when they started the settlement of their regions.) The ceremony was also an acknowledgement of what Joshua certainly considered to have been the principal source of their military success — the unity of the tribes. All were bound by their Covenant with God, by a distinctive faith, and this made the Israel experience so very different from that of other infiltrating nomadic groups who had tried to gain a foothold in Canaan. The Israelites were a more cohesive force than the enemies they faced and were moved by a higher sense of purpose; they accordingly displayed a more tenacious fighting morale. It was their unique faith, as biblical scholar John Bright points out, "which set Israel off from her environment and made her the distinctive and creative phenomenon that she was".

THE TRIBAL CONFEDERACY

The unity forged by Joshua in his lifetime seemed likely to crumble after his death. The army was disbanded as each tribe moved off to its settlement area, and each was soon preoccupied with adapting itself to the new pattern of stable agricultural life and developing its own tribal region. There was no central administration and no central army organization, each tribe maintaining its own militia to protect its own borders. In the absence of an overall leader — there was no successor to Joshua — the tribal elders regained their independent authority, and each tribe tended to plough its own furrow. It was bitterly ironic that the very unity which had brought them such phenomenal success, from bondage in Egypt to almost complete mastery of the Promised Land, should now be squandered. It seemed, indeed, as though the Israelites were reverting to their former separatism, disintegrating into their twelve fragments, each a world unto itself.

If they had been pagan tribes, like the peoples around them, this process would have continued to its logical end, and they would eventually have vanished. However, because of the dramatic event in Sinai, they were now a confederation of tribes bound together by a distinctive code and united in their collective Covenant with God. Added to their common faith was of course the common memory of the awesome wonders of their immediate past. Thus, whatever the degree of autonomy enjoyed by each tribe, all looked up to the central shrine which housed the Ark of the Covenant, and its site was the focal point of the confederacy. Here the tribes would meet in pilgrimage at festival times, and the tribal elders would use the occasion to exchange views on common problems, possibly clear up boundary disputes and perhaps agree to a limited cooperation on matters of mutual interest.

In the initial period of settlement, such exchanges were informal and rarely led to common policy and action of major degree, largely because there was no serious military danger. The two major powers who might have intervened, the Hittite empire in the north and the Egyptian in the south, were now, at the beginning of the 12th century BC, in decline, and the local foes who had been vanquished shortly before had not yet recovered. As for the occasional small-scale raids by marauding nomads, each tribe could cope

The dagger (on the right), and the javelin-head (on the left), discovered at archeological excavations, were in use during the period of Joshua's conquest. (The other weapon, center, belongs to the period of the Patriarchs.)

with these on its own through its tribal militia of veteran warriors.

Within a few decades, however, inter-tribal cooperation became imperative as incursions by formidable new enemies and attacks by old foes who had regained their strength threatened the existence of all the tribes. In the second half of the century came the Philistines from the Aegean region, a hardy people who settled in the unsubdued coastal region and sought to press inland. Then came the Midianites from the desert, using the recently domesticated camel for long-range raids. There was trouble from the Canaanite city-states who had remained unconquered by Joshua. The Aramaeans were infiltrating from Syria. And there was grave military danger from Moam and Ammon, on the east bank of the river Jordan. Some of these peoples hoped to overwhelm the Israelites by gobbling them up tribe by tribe. Instead, though the process was lengthy, they hammered them into national unity.

In times of acute crisis, several tribes would merge their interests and do battle for the common cause, rallying spontaneously behind

The recently discovered water system of Gibeon (El Jib),
six miles northwest of Jerusalem. Archaeology has shown that
the Israelite settlement was responsible for the first intensive
development of the land, particularly of the hill country.
A key factor was their urgent concern with water conservation
and the construction of appropriate water installations.

an *ad hoc* leader. These leaders were known as Judges, and they would lead the people in a campaign either to repel a critical attack or to free a tribal area which had been overrun and put under tribute. In appealing to the other tribes for collective action, they would stress the hazards to all and urge upon them their duties under the Covenant and the need to fight for the survival of the whole community and for the preservation of their faith. They held no formal appointment; they could apply no sanctions if a tribe failed to respond (as many did); and their leadership was temporary. For the most part, when the danger had passed, the Judge would cease to wield authority and the tribes would resume their separate ways — until the next critical threat, and another spontaneous choice of a Judge.

JUDGES
The Judges were drawn from no special tribe, nor even necessarily from the tribal elders. One was a woman. The rest were men who had distinguished themselves in combat and had acquired a reputation beyond their own tribe for outstanding bravery or military ingenuity. All had charisma — the emanation of divine grace — and generated a public feeling that they had been touched by the hand of God. They accordingly commanded a respect and prestige which cut across tribal boundaries, and in moments of peril there would be a popular demand that they accept the reins of leadership.

The account of their deeds appears in the Book of Judges and sheds light on the pattern of Israelite life from the beginning of the 12th to the latter part of the 11th century BC. The biblical Book records the names of twelve. Six receive little more than a mention. The six who figure more prominently are Othniel, Ehud, Deborah, Gideon, Jephthah and Samson, and of these Deborah and Gideon are the most outstanding.

Othniel was the first of the warrior-Judges to be "raised up" by the Lord as "a deliverer for the people of Israel" (Jud. 3:9) when they were being hard-pressed by the northern kingdom of Aram-Naharaim, and he led the tribes to victory. In the days of Ehud the danger came from the east. The Moabites of

A basalt orthostat bearing a relief of a lion, and steles, stone monuments, discovered in the remains of a 14th–13th century BC Canaanite temple at Hazor.

Transjordan had grown in strength and penetrated westwards, across the river. When they reached Jericho, "the city of palms" (Jud. 3:13), Ehud stopped their further encroachment by an act of personal courage which paved the way for a skilful Israelite counterattack.

The peril in Deborah's time came from a group of Canaanite rulers who had banded together under "Jabin king of Canaan" (Jud. 4:2). His commanding general was Sisera, and armed with chariots, which the Israelites lacked, his forces were threatening to seize the valley of Jezreel and cut off the northern tribes from those in the center. Deborah called for joint tribal action, and summoned the outstanding Israelite soldier, Barak, to take command. In the critical confrontation with Sisera, the enemy was vanquished and the threat lifted from Israel. However, this had been effected by only a few of the tribes. Despite the danger, some tribes had failed to respond, and in the victory Song of Deborah (Jud. 5), there is high prise for those who took part in the campaign and withering scorn

It was under a palm tree in the hill country of Ephraim that Deborah the Judge would sit and give counsel to the people of Israel. She played a decisive role in promoting unity among the tribes and at a time of critical danger spurred them to military victory.

for those who stayed away. Unity was still far off.

Gideon, the next Judge, was an inventive military commander and so popular a leader that the people wished to make him king, but he rejected the offer, saying "the Lord will rule over you" (Jud. 8:23). However, the very suggestion that one man be given supreme authority over all the tribes shows that by now, the 11th century, they were beginning to recognize the need for a central administration. In the century or so since they had started their settlement of the country, they had become good farmers, and their growing prosperity brought increased threats from covetous neighbors and distant marauders. It was this, no doubt, that prompted their desire for closer inter-tribal cooperation. It was Gideon's masterly stratagem by the Spring of Harod (described in Jud. 7) which put an end to the annual incursions of the camel-riding Midianites, who would journey north from the southern desert to raid the Israelite granaries at harvest time.

Jephthah was a man of Gilead, the Israelite section of Transjordan, which had been

The archaeological site of biblical Megiddo (below),
a few miles west of Mount Tabor and commanding
a strategic pass at the western end of
the valley of Jezreel, was close to the battlefield
where the crucial clash took place.

invaded by the neighboring Ammonites. Though he was a tough military commander. Jephthah first tried diplomacy to secure a peaceful Ammonite withdrawal — the absorbing exchange between the two sides is recounted in Jud. 11:12–28 — and only when the parleys proved fruitless did he go into action.

Samson was the most colourful of the Judges, but unlike the others he exercised no overall authority. He acted rather as a one-man commando unit, performing individual deeds of rare audacity against the Philistines. They had gained considerable strength since establishing themselves in the coastal plain in the previous century and were harrying the Israelites with frequent border raids — which would eventually develop into all-out war. But there was no concerted action to stop them, and so Samson took matters into his own hand. His spectacular exploits (Jud. 13–16) touched the imagination of his people, and contributed in some measure to their ultimate recognition of the need for national unity.

This period of the Judges was fraught with danger and uncertainty, and the fate of Israel hung frequently in the balance. There were times, as we have seen, when it was questionable whether the tribes would survive or go under; whether they would retain their unique identity or assimilate into the surrounding peoples; whether they would remain faithful to their Covenant and Commandments or adopt the gods of their neighbors; and whether the national goal would override tribal ambitions.

Only with the emergence of the prophet Samuel do we see the beginnings of the consolidation of Israel's religion and nationhood.

Gideon was winnowing wheat when he
received the call which propelled him into
battle command and the subsequent
leadership of his people. In some Arab
villages of Israel today, the ancient methods
of separating the grain from the chaff
are still followed.

The Spring of Harod in the valley of Jezreel, where Gideon conducted his celebrated "water test" and selected 300 picked men from among the thousands who had volunteered. The Spring of Harod is now a National Park.

3. THE RELUCTANT KING-MAKER

The uncertain era of the tribal confederacy was brought to an end under the leadership of Samuel; and it was he who launched Israel on its next crucial stage of development, which was marked, in his lifetime, by the inauguration of the monarchy. Thus, although he is known primarily as the prophet Samuel — and he was assuredly the most important of the early prophets since Moses — he was also the last, and greatest, of the Judges, the only one since the death of Joshua and the beginnings of Israelite settlement in the Promised Land to pull the tribes together and give them central direction over a prolonged period. Indeed, after Moses and Joshua, he was the outstanding leader of the Hebrew people in their formative centuries.

His power and authority sprang from a variety of qualities. Like the earlier Judges, he had charisma (though he was also a Judge in the legal sense, with a regular judicial circuit, as we learn from I Sam. 7:15–17). Like several of them, he was a man of sound judgement and wisdom. But unlike most of the others, he was a figure of spiritual eminence, dedicated to the Lord from birth, and

he was able to interpret the Laws of Moses and lay down the norms of righteous and evil behavior which were respected — if not always accepted — by all. Added to this, he had a firm grasp of political affairs, and though not a military man he was not unfamiliar with the strategy and tactics of warfare. He also possessed a towering personality, and to the people — particularly to the tribal elders — he was an awesome figure. But they gave him their allegiance — thereby abdicating some of their own authority — not only because he possessed a rare combination of virtues but also because the tribes were in grievous difficulties. When Samuel first summoned them to a hilltop gathering at Mizpah, just north of Jerusalem, they came because their morale was at its lowest and they thought that perhaps they might hear words of comfort and hope. They had just experienced a shattering reverse in battle with the Philistines near Aphek and suffered many casualties. But most fearful of all, they had lost the Ark of the Covenant. They had brought it to the battlefield from Shiloh in a moment of desperation and it had been captured by the

*And all Israel...
knew that Samuel was
established as a
prophet of the Lord*

(1 Samuel 3:20)

The hilltop village of Nebi Samuel, overlooking
Jerusalem, linked by tradition to the burial
place of the prophet ("Nebi" in Arabic).

43

Then Samuel said, 'Gather all Israel at Mizpah' *(1 Samuel 7:5)*

enemy. They were in a state of shock when they assembled at Mizpah, and Samuel did little at first to spare their feelings, haranguing them for religious backsliding and hankering after the Canaanite deities. But he then exhorted them to renew their faith and follow the ways of righteousness. When the Philistines, learning that they were at Mizpah, advanced against them, Samuel roused their spirits with a ringing call to arms, adding "I will pray to the Lord for you" (I Sam. 7:5). Following his intercession, the heavens opened and unleashed a violent storm, putting the enemy to confusion. Thereafter, his authority was unchallenged.

It may thus be said that what propelled Samuel into the leadership was the Philistine menace; and it kept him there almost for the rest of his life. For this was the latter part of the 11th century BC and the danger was continuous. It was the gravest danger the Israelites had faced since the conquest, and the struggle was fateful. With the retreat of the Egyptians from the area, it was a question of who would gain hegemony over the country, the Philistines or the tribes of Israel.

The Philistines had consolidated themselves in the coastal plain, had developed a high material culture and were well organized and well-armed. They had advanced from border raids on Israelite settlements and were now pressing inland, with every expectation of subduing the tribes or driving them from the country. They might well have done so had the tribes continued as a group of fragmented autonomies. It was their recognition that their ill-trained and poorly equipped tribal militias, operating individually, stood little chance against the concerted onslaught of the Philistines that prompted them to accept central leadership. Samuel was the natural choice.

THE INFANT SAMUEL

He was born of a humble family in Ramathaim-Zophim in the hill country of Ephraim, but was brought up by the priests in the shrine of Shiloh. His father Elkanah had been in the habit of making an annual pilgrimage to Shiloh accompanied by his two wives, Peninnah, who bore him many children, and childless Hannah, who grieved over her state. During the pilgrimage journey Peninnah

44

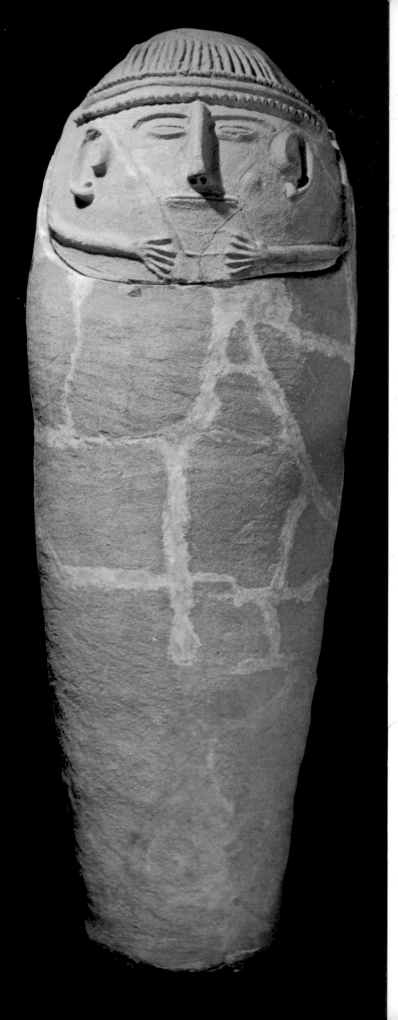

An 11th century BC sarcophagus (left) of the Philistines. Decorative pottery vessels (right) characteristic of Philistine art and workmanship. Such artefacts were found in Israel only at archaeological excavations of sites where the Philistines had dwelt.

would taunt her about her barrenness, and on one occasion, Hannah went into the shrine and vowed in silent prayer that if she were granted a son "then I will give him to the Lord all the days of his life" (I Sam. 1:11). Eli the priest observed the distraught woman and thought she was drunk. But when she explained her anxieties, he comforted her and led her to hope that her petition would be granted. In due time the infant Samuel was born, and when he was weaned, his mother brought him to Shiloh, and there "the boy ministered to the Lord, in the presence of Eli the priest" (I Sam. 2:11).

The tragedy of Eli's declining years were his two sons, Hophni and Phinehas. They, too, were priests, but they were corrupt in their behavior and delinquent in their duties. It was probably on this account that Eli must have lavished special love and instruction on the child who had so unexpectedly come into his life. Certain it is that under Eli's tutelage, "the boy Samuel continued to grow in stature and in favour with the Lord and with men" (I Sam. 2:26). It was during this time that Samuel also heard the direct voice of God,

for the Lord revealed himself to Samuel at Shiloh *(1 Samuel 3:21)*

These are considered to be the remains of an ancient synagogue, discovered at excavations of the archaeological site of Shiloh where the Ark of the Law was kept. Samuel was brought as an infant to this central shrine and grew up within its precincts as the ward of Eli the Priest.

"for the Lord revealed himself to Samuel at Shiloh" (I Sam. 3:21).

Living within the precincts of the central shrine, and as the ward of Eli, Samuel would have been a familiar figure from childhood to all people who came to Shiloh for the pilgrim festivals — and particularly to the elders of all the tribes. For they would pay their respects to Eli, and take a fond interest in the lad at his side. As he grew older, they would share Eli's pride in his progress; and they would be struck by the marked difference in learning, integrity and bearing between him and the two disreputable sons of the priest. He must have emerged as an impressive young man — and the tribal leaders would remember this later when they found themselves in critical straits.

PHILISTINE MENACE
Not since the time of Joshua did the tribes of Israel now face so grave and extensive a military problem. It is not that they were unused to attack. Throughout their settling-in period of the previous century and a half, they were rarely free of raids and assaults.

48

Now Israel went out to battle against the Philistines *(1 Samuel 4:1)*

The coastal plain, where the Philistines
had consolidated themselves
and were proving a sore menace
to the Israelite tribes settled inland.

But these either presented only a limited threat, with which an individual tribe could cope alone, or, when there was danger to all, it was usually a one-time danger which could be banished in a decisive blow struck by the tribes acting together under the temporary leadership of a Judge. Now, however, for the first time, the situation was not one which could be altered by victory in a single battle. They were under the perpetual threat of a powerful people whose aim was nothing less than conquest, and what was at stake was their very existence — life, land, religion, identity. A loose organization of autonomous tribes was no match for this new type of enemy with its new and ominous designs. Nor was another Judge the answer if, like his predecessors, he was neither to possess formal authority nor allowed to apply sanctions. What the Israelites needed was a leader with official powers who would make them operate as a concerted unit, welding the tribes together, drawing upon the tribal militias to raise a national army, planning the overall strategy and determining military policy. Only such central organization and leadership

could enable the Israelites to meet the vigorous and ambitious Philistines with any chance of eventual victory — and, in the opening phases, at least of holding their own. But they were to go through a long and dark period before they realized it — in time to take appropriate action. The event which started to open their eyes was their defeat near Aphek, at the edge of the coastal plain.

In the first stage of the battle, the Philistines emerged the victors. This so dispirited the tribal elders that they sent to Shiloh for the Ark to be brought to the battlefield before putting in a counter-attack. Hophni and Phinehas arrived with it and its presence did wonders to the morale of the Israelite troops. Indeed, their uninhibited rejoicing was such that its sounds reached the encampment of the Philistines, plunging them into gloom. But the Philistines were well led, and their officers promptly roused them with a fiery do-not-be-dismayed talk, urging them to "Take courage, and acquit yourselves like men" (I Sam. 4:9). The Israelites had the Ark but not the leadership, and when battle was again joined, they were utterly routed. Eli's sons were among

Let the ark of the God of Israel be brought around to Gath

(1 Samuel 5:8)

The ancient site of Gath, one of the cities to which the Israelite Ark of the Law was taken by the Philistines who had captured it in battle, but who were so plagued by its possession that they cast it from their midst.

the large numbers who were killed, and the Ark was captured. The sole Israelite consolation, meager and temporary, was that possession of the Ark proved an unending torment to the Philistines. They took it gleefully to the temple of Dagon in Ashdod — and their idol tumbled onto its face. When this was followed by a plague, there was an outcry for the Ark to be removed, and it was taken to Gath. The plague followed, and it was carried to Ekron. Eventually, the wise Philistine leaders decided to cast it from their midst and it was despatched to Kiriath-Jearim — on the hill above today's Abu Ghosh, a few miles west of Jerusalem, and a border village at the time — where it lay in neglect for twenty years.

The Philistines, however, had captured more than the Ark after Aphek. They now occupied enclaves within Israel territory in the central hill country, held much of the Jezreel Valley and parts of the northern Negev, and they proceeded to establish garrisons at key centres (as is recorded in I Sam. 10:5 and 13:3). They also captured Shiloh and destroyed the shrine which had held the Ark.

(This we know from archaeological excavations carried out at the site, though there is no specific record in the Book of Samuel. There is however a hint of it in Jeremiah 7:12 and 26:6.)

The Israelites were in utter disarray. Their central shrine was gone — and with it the unofficial "capital" of the tribal federation and meeting place of their elders. Eli, the priest of Shiloh, had collapsed and died on hearing that the Ark had been captured and his two sons killed. The tribal militias had been mauled and the survivors of the Aphek debacle had straggled home, so that there was no central force for the moment. Yet the danger was still with them, for the Philistines, full of confidence after their successes, seemed determined to exploit their advantage and press on with their aim of conquest. The Israelites were in despair.

It was in this bitter situation that the prophet Samuel emerged to rally them at Mizpah, his powerful appeal lifting them out of their despondency and directing them into constructive action. When this was followed by a Philistine attack which was vigorously

52

repulsed and the Philistines were chased from the area, the Israelites could enjoy a period of relative calm. Samuel was their undisputed leader. With Shiloh destroyed, Samuel went to live in Ramah, some six miles north of Jerusalem, and from there "he administered justice to Israel" (I Sam. 7:17). But he also "went on a circuit year by year to Bethel, Gilgal, and Mizpah; and he judged Israel in all those places" (I Sam. 7:16). It is evident that since there was now no Shiloh, no central shrine and no tribal centre, Samuel made it his business to go round the country visiting the tribes and, in addition to administering justice, encouraging the people and strengthening their faith in God — and in themselves. At the same time, he would review the political and military situation and discuss policy with the tribal elders. It is likely that as a result of such visits, there would be armed forays from individual tribes against the Philistine enclaves.

Certain it is that the prophet Samuel was the galvanizing force during this sombre Israelite period, and that the spirit of armed resistance, which leapt into sporadic flame, was maintained throughout. There was now greater inter-tribal cooperation than before, thanks to Samuel. But the political framework and the administrative pattern were still the same, with secular authority confined to the tribal leaders and wielded on a patriarchal basis. Samuel enjoyed no formal powers, and though he was looked up to by all the tribes because of his stature and his moral authority as the instrument of the Lord, he had always to lead by persuasion.

This might have been sufficient if the Israelites had only to mark time in order to survive. But the Philistine menace was becoming sharper week by week. The five main Philistine kingdoms of Gaza, Ashdod, Gath, Ashkelon and Ekron had shown that they could act in concert with remarkable success, and they could put a unified army in the field. They had now fashioned a powerful military organization based on the chariot, and their support infantry were equipped with locally manufactured weapons which were far superior to anything in the Israelite arsenal. They were made of iron, and the Philistines were careful to guard their secret and their monopoly: "Now there was no smith to be found throughout all the land of Israel; for the Philistines said, 'Lest the Hebrews make themselves swords or spears' . . . So . . . there was neither sword nor spear found in the hand of any of the [Israelite] people . . ." (I Sam. 13: 19, 22).

"GIVE US A KING"

The Philistines still occupied much if not all of the Israelite territory they had captured and occupied shortly before Samuel appeared on the scene; and Samuel had done well so far in stopping the rot, preventing further encroachments and even encouraging occasional raids. But even holding on to what they had was becoming precarious in face of the growing Philistine might; and as for dealing the enemy a decisive blow which would liberate the tribal territories, this was beyond the capacity of a fractionized community. To achieve this, the Israelites would need to introduce a formal centralized leadership and institute closer tribal unity. This had assuredly been urged upon the tribal elders by Samuel, but he could never have imagined that

their final acceptance of his recommendations would take the form it did.

When, after lengthy discussions among themselves, they eventually concluded that the pressures were urgent and that none of the individual tribes was a match for the Philistines, they all proceeded in a body to Ramah, entered the presence of the great Samuel, and said to him: "Give us a king to govern us" (I Sam. 8:6). Samuel was outraged, particularly as they had added that they wanted to be governed by a king "like all the nations". Israel was not — nor was her purpose to be — like the other nations at that time, with their pagan gods and their flesh and blood kings. Monarchy was totally alien to the Israelite tradition, for the king of the Hebrews was the Lord himself, and he exercised his guidance through his prophets or Judges. Why insert another personage between God's prophets and God's people? Samuel was no doubt pleased that the elders finally come round to realizing the need for tribal unity. But why then, he must have wondered privately, did they demand another supra-tribal leader when they already had

the ark was lodged at Kiriath-Jearim... some twenty years

(1 Samuel 7:2)

Kiriat-Jearim (today's Abu Ghosh) where
the Ark of the Law was finally sent by
the Philistines after this battle trophy had
caused them endless suffering. Twenty
years later king David brought the Ark
to Jerusalem.

Samuel himself, their divine prophet and
guide? The elders, wise in the ways of men,
had anticipated his unspoken thought. "Behold", they said to him, "you are old and
your sons do not walk in your ways" (I Sam.
8:5). None of Samuel's children was of a
calibre to succeed him, and who would lead
them when Samuel died? Better to choose
someone now, while Samuel, though old, was
still alive, and could give the new man his
blessing and advice. They wanted a young
man. Above all they wanted a fighting commander. Samuel sought divine guidance, and
the Lord told him to agree.

The man chosen to be king was Saul, the
son of Kish, of Gibeah, and he was "a hand-
some young man ... from his shoulders up-
ward he was taller than any of the people"
(I Sam. 9:2). He belonged to the tribe of
Benjamin, whose territory was close to the
area of Philistine danger, and was also located
in the centre of the country. These factors
may have favored the choice of a Benjaminite.
Moreover, Benjamin was one of the smallest
tribes, and the honor that would accrue to
it was likely to excite fewer jealousies. But

undoubtedly the key virtue of Saul in the
eyes of the elders at this time was that he
had shown himself to be a first class soldier,
having just inflicted a stunning defeat on
the Ammonites at Jabesh-Gilead, across the
Jordan, with a display of brilliant and charismatic generalship. Indeed, in the biblical
account of this battle (I Sam. 11), Saul
reveals the kind of qualities (not unlike those
of Gideon) which, in an earlier generation,
would have qualified him as a Judge.

The Bible gives two varying accounts of
the royal inauguration (I Sam. 8–12). One
presents the charming story of Saul's private
anointment by Samuel at Ramah and his
subsequent confirmation by public acclamation at Gilgal after his victory over the Ammonites. This account is uncritical of the
monarchy. The second describes his selection
by lot, conducted by a protesting Samuel,
and acclamation at Mizpah, and is outspoken-
ly anti-monarchic. It seems evident from
much of the text and also from the later
relationship between the prophet and the king
that Samuel was vehemently against the idea
of kingship, and remained so to his dying

Ancient weights from the Israelite period inscribed
with Hebrew terms marking their various denominations.
They were based on the weight of the Shekel,
which was the equivalent of 11 grams.
The unit marked with the Hebrew "Pym", for example,
was two thirds of a Shekel-weight – just over 7 grams.

day; but the tribal leaders insisted that only a monarch could save them in their desperate situation, and he finally gave way. Incidentally, both narratives present Samuel in the key role of "king-maker", however reluctant, and, driven to choose, he chose Saul.

At one point in the tough negotiations which preceded the royal appointment, Samuel set out his views on kingship, and it remains to this day a classic statement against monarchy:

"These will be the ways of the king who will reign over you: he will take your sons and appoint them to his chariots and to be his horsemen . . . and he will appoint for himself commanders . . . and some to plough his ground and to reap his harvest, and to make his implements of war . . . He will take your daughters to be perfumers and cooks and bakers. He will take the best of your fields and vineyards and olive orchards and give them to his servants. He will take the tenth of your grain and your vineyards and give it to his officers and to his servants. He will take your menservants and maidservants, and the best of your cattle and your asses, and

put them to his work. He will take the tenth of your flocks, and you shall be his slaves" (I Sam. 8:10–17).

But the people remained unmoved. These were grave words and full of wisdom, but they contained no answer to the immediate Philistine threat. They wanted a king who would "go out before us and fight our battles" (I Sam. 8:20).

SAUL THE WARRIOR-MONARCH

Saul proved to be just the man for that, and he was, indeed, to spend the rest of his life in battle. His kingship changed little in the broad administrative pattern of Israelite society — except where it impinged on defence matters. The normal day-to-day non-military affairs of the tribes were conducted as before by the tribal leaders. Saul was of course in constant touch with them, but he established no central government. Unlike the neighboring monarchs — and many of his successors — he built no lavish palaces, presided over no stately courts, set his face against high living. (Evidence of his austerity was brought to light at archaeological exca-

I will send to you a man from the land of Benjamin, and you shall anoint him to be prince over my people Israel (1 Samuel 9:16)

The territory of the tribe of Benjamin, in the centre of the country, close to the area of Philistine danger at the time of Samuel. Saul, a member of this tribe, was chosen to be the first king of Israel.

vations which showed that the Gibeah of his day — his hometown base — held only structures of the utmost simplicity.)

Saul was solely concerned with warfare — the preservation of Israel's security against the threats and pressures of the Philistines — and he reorganized the military structure of the tribal community to meet the new, continuing challenge. He was the first to raise the nucleus of a regular army, with the individual tribal militias kept in reserve, able to continue with their civilian labors but immediately on call in time of national emergency. (This is the broad principle applied in the Israel Defence Forces today, which maintain a comparatively small regular army together with the young men and women on national service, while the bulk of the able-bodied population go about their normal functions but are speedily mobilized when the country is threatened.) Saul's small regular army had the functions of dealing with minor raids, holding the line in major attacks until the tribal levies could be mobilized, serving as cadres for the fully called-up forces, and spear-heading major assaults. Responsibility

for provisioning the troops in the field lay with their own clans and tribes. In the biblical preamble to David's duel with Goliath, we read that when the tribal levies who had been called up by Saul were in the field against the Philistines, "Jesse said to David his son, 'Take for your brothers an ephah of this parched grain, and these ten loaves, and carry them quickly to the camp to your brothers; also take these ten cheeses to the commander of their thousand' " (I Sam. 17:17–18). This was the practice also followed in the pre-Saul period. The penultimate chapter in Judges relates that when the Israelites were about to attack a certain city, they said: "we will go up against it by lot, and we will take ten men of a hundred throughout all the tribes of Israel, and a hundred of a thousand, and a thousand of ten thousand, to bring provisions for the people" (Judges 20:9–10).

Yigael Yadin points out that Saul used the tactical structure of the three unit formation, and went in for night marches, to effect surprise, with attack at dawn. These moves are well seen in the biblical record of Saul's earlier battle with Ammon at Jabesh-Gilead:

61

An ivory tusk belonging to the middle of the 1st millennium BC
found at Megiddo, similar in outline to the horn-shaped
vessel used in the anointing ceremony of the ancient kings.

"And on the morrow Saul put the people in
three companies; and they came into the
midst of the camp in the morning watch, and
cut down the Ammonites until the heat of
the day" — that is, from dawn till noon.
Yadin writes that Saul's division of his forces
into three groups was "the most convenient
formation for manoeuvre in different situa-
tions: one company on a fixed front, with a
company on either side; two companies fixed
and one on a flank; or two companies committed and one held in reserve". This was
also the disposition of his forces in his later
battles against the Philistines, and in a reference to an engagement where Saul used only
his select, regular force without requiring his
main reserves of tribal levies, the Bible records that "Saul chose three thousand men
of Israel; two thousand were with Saul . . .
and a thousand were with Jonathan . . . and
the rest of the people he sent home, every
man to his tent" (I Sam. 13:2).

Saul did not conquer the Philistines nor
destroy their capacity to make war; but he
succeeded in the mission for which he had
been made king by driving the Philistines

oil, and anointed him (1 Samuel 16:13)

from the central hill country back to the coastal plain and liberating much of Israelite territory. For a good while thereafter, the engagements with the enemy took place mostly in the border area at the periphery of the plain. He therefore did much in the early years of his reign to neutralize the Philistine threat.

His most important victory after becoming king was at the battle of Michmash. The engagement had been going badly, but the tide turned after a remarkable deed of personal valour by Saul's son Jonathan, described in I Sam. 14. Michmash commanded an important pass in the central hills, a few miles northeast of Gibeah, where Saul maintained his fortified operational base, and it was perhaps the key centre within Israelite territory which the Philistines had captured earlier and continued to occupy. It had to be regained if the tribal lands were to be liberated, and after launching a series of raids on several nearby Philistine garrisons, in which Jonathan took a prominent part, Saul mobilized his forces and did battle with the enemy at the pass of Michmash. The Philistines were routed, and the Israelites gained not simply a breathing spell but a new lease of hope in their future.

A PROPHET'S ANGER

Saul did well, but he had a hard time throughout his reign, buffeted in the early years by the anger of the prophet Samuel and in the later years by the rivalry of the popular young David. But even from the biblical account, in which his meritorious record is squeezed between the greatness of these two men, Saul emerges as a talented, dedicated and appealing figure, the ideal commander for the conditions of the times.

Samuel's eminence was as great as ever and his spiritual authority was accepted even by Saul. He was still the guide and teacher of his people, still the man of God and the repository of the public conscience, seeking always to steer them along the paths of righteousness. However, he had never reconciled himself to the monarchy, despite the reluctant approval by the Lord, and he still considered it a blasphemy. He was angry with the people and the tribal leaders for demanding it, yet

the messengers came to Gibeah of Saul *(1 Samuel 11:4)*

Tel el Ful, site of ancient Gibeah, the hometown base of king Saul. It is today a suburb on the northern outskirts of Jerusalem.

he seemed to direct his fury mainly at Saul, even though Saul had not sought the position and had indeed been anointed by Samuel himself. The impression is inescapable, since Samuel's bitterness became more marked after Saul's successes, that his was the natural resentment of the aged ex-leader towards his young and victorious successor — though Saul thought himself more disciple than successor to the great Samuel. Saul was no docile puppet, and in the military sphere he was every inch the commander; but he was careful to consult with Samuel before a major engagement, and hearken with respect to his hypercritical mentor who became increasingly censorious. At one stage in their relationship, when Saul was about to attack the Philistines and Samuel failed to appear at the appointed time to offer the ritual sacrifices, Saul offered them himself, since any further delay would have been dangerous. Samuel turned up soon after and was so angry that he abruptly informed Saul that "your kingdom shall not continue" and "the Lord has sought out a man after his own heart" (I Sam. 13:14) who would replace him. It says much for

The anointment of David by Samuel,
depicted in one of the striking wall paintings
of biblical scenes in the 3rd century synagogue
of Dura-Europos on the river Euphrates.

Now Saul... and all the men of Israel, were in the valley of Elah, fighting with the Philistines *(1 Samuel 17:19)*

The valley of Elah where the young David fought his duel with the giant Goliath while the rival Israel and Philistine armies stood arrayed on the opposing hillsides.

Saul that despite this staggering blow to his confidence, he went ahead and won the battle with the Philistines.

Samuel's final break with the king came after Saul's victory over the Amalekites. They had been raiding the northern Negev, and Saul had by now established sufficient stability in the central region to be able to mobilize a considerable force and rush south to deal a crushing blow to the attackers. Before leaving, Samuel had relayed to him the divine instructions to wipe them all out and take no booty, but Saul had spared the life of the enemy king, Agag, taking him captive, and his men had brought back the choicest of their herds and flocks. Samuel denounced him bitterly for disobeying the Lord's instructions. He had Agag brought forth and killed him with his own hand, saying: "As your sword has made women childless, so shall your mother be childless among women" (I Sam. 15:33). He then left Saul without ceremony for Ramah and never again did the two meet. However, Samuel was not without compassion, for the Bible adds: "but Samuel grieved over Saul". Shortly thereafter, he was in-structed by the Lord to proceed to Bethlehem and anoint the young lad David as the future king.

Though on the face of it Samuel's attitude to Saul seems to have been prompted by jealously, there was also a deep-seated non-personal reason — the fear that the king, who symbolized the new secular order which was replacing the old (an early form of the Church v. State conflict), was also seeking to usurp priestly authority. The two main outbursts of the prophet's fury came when Saul made the ritual sacrifice before battle and later when he ignored the religious in-structions concerning the Amalekites. This, Samuel felt, threatened the very core of Isra-elite society, its faith, and what followed was the public intimation that Saul no longer enjoyed divine approbation.

The impact on Saul was tragic. From now on, he seemed to move without a compass, bereft of Samuel's sustaining spirit, and con-scious, too, of the effect of Samuel's disavowal upon the tribal elders. Yet the Philistine danger was still urgent and this was Saul's primary responsibility. But whereas previous-

the Philistines... found Saul... fallen on Mount Gilboa... and they fastened his body to the wall of Beth-shan (1 Samuel 30:8-10)

The archaeological hill in the background holds the ruins of Beth Shan. Upon the walls of this city the Philistines displayed the bodies of king Saul and his sons after the Israelite defeat at the battle of Mount Gilboa.

ly he had met it with courage and high confidence, he was now smitten with doubt; and even when he was successful, the glory went to another — which further eroded his confidence and affected his judgement. With his next big victory, for example, it was the prelude with Goliath which was acclaimed, and it was the young David who carried off the honors from the field of battle. The biblical record then shows Saul spending almost as much time chasing David as he spent pursuing the Philistines.

Nor did the death of Samuel liberate Saul from his anguished conscience. In the last days of his reign, the Philistines gathered a large army and advanced into the valley of Jezreel. Saul mobilized and encamped opposite them on Mount Gilboa. But he had lost heart, and in his desperation he left camp in disguise one night and went to seek out a noted medium in the hamlet of Endor, in the valley of Jezreel between Gilboa and Mount Tabor. He asked the woman to summon up the spirit of Samuel, and Saul then heard the familiar, gruff, unrelenting voice of the prophet demanding "Why have you disturbed me by bringing me up?" (I Sam. 28:15). Saul said he was in great distress with the Philistines and that "God has turned away from me and answers me no more". The voice of Samuel confirmed that the Lord had indeed rejected him because of his religious disobedience, and added the prediction that the Israelites would be defeated, and Saul and his sons would die, in the battle next day. The already disconsolate Saul was now utterly distraught, hardly the ideal mood for a commander about to go into action, and his army was indeed beaten. He, however, died with dignity. His three sons, including Jonathan, were killed, and he was wounded by an enemy archer. He asked his armor-bearer to finish him off, and when the aide refused, "Saul took his own sword, and fell upon it" (I Sam. 31:4).

This key battle on the slopes of Mount Gilboa might have been a turning point in the fortunes of the two peoples, with the Israelites plummeting to the depths and the Philistines riding the crest, if it had not been for the young man of the tribe of Judah whom Samuel had anointed. David, who had not participated in this fateful battle with the Philistines, had built up an elite force of his own and had already amassed considerable fighting — and diplomatic — experience since the day he had faced Goliath.

This popular military hero, tough but also poetic, devout but also earthy — some of his foibles were as egregious as his virtues — and with charisma as the designate of God and the man blessed by Samuel, would in a few years become the favored leader of all the Israelites. Thanks to the accomplishments of Samuel and Saul, as well as to his own qualities, he would succeed in amalgamating the tribes as they had never been joined since the days of Joshua, and in securing their acceptance of his supreme political and military authority. He would carry the fighting with the Philistines over to their territory, crush their offensive capability, and make Israel united, safe and strong.

King David, as portrayed in the 13th
century illuminated Armenian Bible of
Erzincan, in the Library of
St. Thoros, Jerusalem.

4. THE FIERY SEERS

It was now the 9th century BC, and Israel was neither united nor strong — nor safe. The nation had reached extraordinary peaks under David and Solomon in the previous century; but now all seemed to be disintegrating — nationhood, state and religion. There might well have been a general collapse if it had not been for the courageous words and activities of two formidable personalities, the great prophet Elijah and his disciple and successor Elisha. If the 11th century BC may be said to have belonged to Samuel and Saul, the 10th century to David and Solomon, the 9th was the century of Elijah and Elisha for their impact on the northern kingdom of Israel.

THE ILLUSTRIOUS DAVID

King David had consolidated Jewish nationhood in its own land and restored its unique religion as the centre of Jewish life. He captured Jerusalem, the Jebusite enclave which had separated the southern from the northern tribes, and proclaimed this centrally located city as the political capital, an utterly new feature in the administration of the tribes. He next brought the Ark of the Covenant from Kiriath-Jearim to Jerusalem, so that the political centre also became the religious capital of the nation. He acquired a site for it on the highest spot in this hill-city, the traditional Mount Moriah, which at the time was the "threshing floor of Araunah the Jebusite" (II Sam. 24:18). He had insisted on buying this plot although it was offered him as a gift, and upon it, to house the Ark, he erected a tent-like structure, underlining its link with the nomad's tent which had covered the shrine in the Sinai desert. Establishing the Tabernacle within the administrative capital did much to bind the tribes to Jerusalem and strengthen their political unity.

David firmly secured the frontiers of a united Israel by a judicious combination of diplomatic alliances and a series of successful campaigns against the Philistines and other threatening neighbors, who were put under tribute. During his reign, Israel became the most powerful State in the territory which lay between Assyria in the northeast and Egypt in the southwest. Subduing the Philistines gave him control of the Mediterranean coastal plain. Capture of Damascus and cities

further north brought his dominions up to the Euphrates. His eastern frontiers took in Transjordan, and his southern territories gave him an outlet to the Red Sea through the Gulf of Eilat.

SOLOMON'S TEMPLE

His son and successor, king Solomon, reaped the full benefits of these military and political achievements, and with no external threats and therefore no battles to fight, he could apply himself wholly to preserving the military and diplomatic accomplishments of his father and to advancing the material prosperity of the nation. He built up a formidable army establishment, based on the chariot. He also fortified strategic centers and set up military bases. On the diplomatic front, he strengthened the alliances contracted by his father, notably with Hiram of Tyre, which was the most important, and forged new ones. Among the latter was the amicable relationship with Egypt, judiciously furthered by his marriage to the pharaoh's daughter. (John Bright says: "This illustrates both the relative importance of Israel and the low estate to which Egypt had sunk: Pharaohs of the Empire did not give their daughters even to kings of Babylon or Mitanni!") In the economic sphere, Solomon "built a fleet of ships" (I Kgs. 9:26), conducted a thriving maritime trade, and developed the copper industry.

But his most spectacular achievement, in terms of its impact on the unity — and history — of his people, was the construction of "the house of the Lord" (I Kings 6:1), the Temple, upon the site where his father had erected the Tabernacle. Though it was a sumptuous structure, the interior conformed to the traditional simplicity with which the Hebrews had launched and nurtured their new faith. This was the only contemporary religion, as we have seen, which fashioned no material shape or image of God. The heart of the Temple was the "oracle", a gloomy cubicle containing the Ark, which from the days of Sinai was "inhabited" by the Supreme Being. "There was nothing in the ark except the two tables of stone which Moses put there at Horeb, where the Lord made a covenant with the people of Israel" (I Kings 8:9). And at the inauguration, after the Ark was

The tomb located on the traditional site of David's burial place on Jerusalem's Mount Zion, a shrine which has drawn Jewish pilgrims throughout the ages.

reverently placed in the darkness of the inner chamber, it came to pass that "when the priests came out of the holy place, a cloud filled the house of the Lord" (I Kings 8:10). The people of Israel, assembled in the sunlit court outside, turned towards the sombre, imageless shrine and worshipped the divine presence, while Solomon pronounced the nature of the One God. Through his words and those of the later prophets, the Temple and the city of Jerusalem, Mount Zion, were to be invested with a unique sacredness, fount of the Jewish religion and central inspiration of the Jewish nation, which would last long after the Temple structure was destroyed and throughout all the centuries of Jewish exile, right down to our own day.

Thus, during the first eighty years of the 10th century BC, spanning the reigns of David and Solomon, the nation of Israel attained its greatest unity and reached the height of its glory. The tribes of Israel were now the nation of Israel and they were in full possession of the land of Israel which had been promised to the Patriarchs. The historic undertaking of resistance, freedom and inde-

The Gulf of Eilat at dawn. Solomon's
kingdom extended southwards to Ezion Geber,
at the head of the gulf, where the king
"built a fleet of ships".

pendence launched by Moses had now been
fulfilled. Nationhood and faith were inte-
grated, and both were now inalienably linked
with Zion. This link, whether physical or
spiritual, would last — and be as vibrant
three thousand years later as it was then.

THE DIVIDED KINGDOM

But it did not seem so in the year 922 BC
when Solomon died; for with his death everything fell apart. No one at the time would
have predicted that the Jews could survive
as a people with a specific identity and with
a specific faith. The collapse of the united
kingdom was due in no small measure to
Solomon himself. Great as he was, he had
his shortcomings, and he showed a singular
lack of foresight in his drastic taxation policy
and the exaction of forced labor for his building projects. He had been strong enough,
however, to keep disgruntled groups in check;
but when he died, the kingdom split. The
northern tribes revolted, seceded and established their own state, which was called Israel.
Jerusalem now remained the capital of a
truncated state to the south, called Judah,

77

which continued the Davidic line. In place of the former single, united and vigorous kingdom, there were now two small, weak, quarrelsome states, and for the next fity years the two were at intermittent war with each other. This civil strife could give comfort and opportunity only to their hostile neighbors, and the territories which had formed part of the Israel empire and which had been under tribute to David and Solomon broke away. The fortunes, political, economic and spiritual, of both Israel and Judah went into decline, the moral laxness and drift towards idolatry being particularly marked in the northern state.

Not until the reign of Omri (876–869 BC), who reached the Israel throne in the final years of king Asa of Judah, were there the beginnings of a rapprochement between the two rival branches of the Israelite stem. It was Omri, incidentally, who resolved to establish a capital in Israel which could vie, at least in the temporal realm, with Jerusalem, the capital of Judah. He therefore "bought the hill of Samaria from Shemer for two talents of silver; and he fortified the hill, and

called the name of the city which he built, Samaria" (I Kings 16:24). (It was renamed Sebaste by Herod some nine centuries later.) It was located on the western face of Mount Ephraim, close to Shechem (today's Nablus) and commanding the principal pass in the area to the Mediterranean coast, twenty-three miles to the west. Upon this noble site, Omri and his successor, Ahab, carried out magnificent construction works, and the remains may be seen today.

Omri sought to revive the material, if not the religious, fortunes of his land, and for this he needed peaceful borders. Moreover, if he could conclude a non-aggression pact with his southern neighbor, Judah, this would lessen the danger of attack by his Syrian neighbor in the north. However, neither he nor Asa lived long enough to complete their peace arrangements. This was achieved by their sons, Ahab of Israel, who came to the throne in 869 BC, and Jehoshaphat of Judah, who became king in 873. Despite their wide differences in character and religious outlook, both, for their own reasons, wanted an end to hostilities, and "Jehoshaphat . . . made

For the king had a fleet of ships of Tarshish at sea… bringing gold, silver, ivory, apes, and peacocks *(1 Kings 10:22)*

Model of a Phoenician cargo vessel, based on an ancient mural, prototype of the "ships of Tarshish" which were the mainstay of Solomon's commercial fleet.

The isle of Jezirat Fara'oun
in the Gulf of Eilat, Solomon's
outlet to the Red Sea.

Gate of Ahab's citadel within the city of Hazor
which Solomon had rebuilt in the previous
century. This gate is a reconstruction from
its original stones which were discovered at
recent archaeological excavations.

peace with the king of Israel" (I Kings 22:44).

In the twenty-four years of his reign in Judah, Jehoshaphat proved to be an inspiring influence. He was a devout king who advanced the cause of justice throughout the land of Judah. By violent contrast, the kingdom of Israel, during the nineteen year reign of king Ahab, was rife with injustice and rampant with paganism. In furtherance of his policy of establishing close commercial ties with the Phoenicians, Omri had arranged for his son Ahab to marry "Jezebel the daughter of Ethbaal king of the Sidonians (I Kings 16:31). Jezebel was a worshipper of the Phoenician god Baal Melkart and of Asherah (the name denotes either a goddess or else a sacred tree or a wooden pillar associated with fertility rites). When she married, she was allowed to bring the images of her deities with her, together with her priests and retainers, and to continue her religious practices in Israel. For this purpose, Ahab "erected an altar for Baal" in a pagan temple "which he built in Samaria" (I Kings 16:32), and when Jezebel became queen, she secured offi-

cial status for "the four hundred and fifty prophets of Asherah" (I Kings 18:19) and maintained them as part of her household. She was clearly a dominating personality and was determined to impose her alien gods and imported heathen customs upon court and country, with the aid — or passive unconcern — of Ahab. Devout Israelites were persecuted and protesting priests and prophets were executed, forced into hiding or driven out.

ELIJAH'S TRIUMPH
It is against this background of tense religious crisis, with the acute danger of Israel's faith being smothered by paganism and the nation crumbling through assimilation into the surrounding pagan groups, that the prophet Elijah appears on the scene, rallying the pious and the ambivalent, forcing a climactic confrontation between the followers of Baal and the followers of God, halting the spread of Jezebel's influence and preserving the supremacy of the Hebrew faith. Elijah's triumph symbolizes the victory of monotheism in its constant struggle against the seductive and erosive temptations of paganism.

83

We first find him, a wild unkempt figure, clad in a loin cloth and a hair cloak, storming into the presence of king Ahab, castigating him with bitter words and crying out warnings of doom: "As the Lord the God of Israel lives, before whom I stand, there shall be neither dew nor rain these years, except by my word" (I Kings 17:1). Before the astonished monarch could have him arrested, Elijah escaped, hurrying eastwards and crossing the Jordan to be out of reach of the vengeful Jezebel.

Of his early years we know nothing, the Bible telling us only that he was "Elijah the Tishbite, of Tishbe in Gilead", the mountainous district east of the river Jordan. After his first dramatic self-invited "audience" with the king, he went into hiding — it was to become a frequent practice after every one of his tempestuous outbursts — near "the brook Cherith" until its water dried up "because there was no rain in the land" (I Kings 17:5, 7). The severe drought which was to grip the kingdom had started.

The next biblical episodes show Elijah as the instrument of divine miracles. Told by the Lord to cross the border into Phoenician territory and proceed to Zarephath, a Mediterranean coastal village a few miles south of Sidon, where "I have commanded a widow there to feed you" (I Kings 17:9), Elijah finds the poor woman gathering sticks. But she has no food to spare. All she has is a little flour in a jar and a little oil, and she is collecting the kindling to cook the last meal for herself and her young son before dying of starvation. Elijah reassures her — and the flour and oil last the three of them until the end of the drought.

Elijah lodged with them in an upstairs room, and one day the boy fell ill and died. The mother was distraught. Elijah jicked up the boy, took him up to his room and laid him on his own bed. He then stretched out upon the body of the lad three times, praying to God to restore him to life. The boy was resuscitated. (A similar miracle, associated with the prophet Elisha, is recounted in II Kings 4.)

Then came the critical confrontation with the false prophets of Jezebel. When the drought, already in its third year, was about

Omri... bought the hill of Samaria from Shemer... and he fortified the hill, and called the name of the city which he built, Samaria, after the name of Shemer (1 Kings 16:23-24)

The "hill of Samaria", which gave its name to the city built upon it by king Omri of Israel in the 9th century BC. These ruins on the site belong to a later age. Samaria was rebuilt by Herod in the 1st century BC and renamed Sebaste.

to break, Elijah was instructed by the Lord to leave Zarephath for the kingdom of Israel and see Ahab again. Entering Samaria, he came across Obadiah, the royal chamberlain, who had been sent by Ahab on a reconnaissance tour through the parched land to search for some green patches of pasture. A pious man — he saved and hid a hundred priests whom Jezebel had ordered executed, and he was full of reverence for Elijah — he told the prophet that he was a "wanted" man; the king had hunted him everywhere, and he implied that he should now make himself scarce. He was horrified when Elijah said that, far from running away, he had come specifically to see the king, and more so when he told the chamberlain to notify Ahab that he was on his way. Obadiah feared that this would cost him his own life, and it took much persuasion before he finally agreed.

Ahab came out to meet Elijah with the words: "Is it you, you troubler of Israel?" Elijah retorted: "I have not troubled Israel; but you have, and your father's house, because you have forsaken the commandments of the Lord and followed the Baals" (I Kings

Part of the archaeological site of Megiddo overlooking the valley of Jezreel where king Ahab owned a winter estate and where queen Jezebel went to such cruel lengths to secure the neighboring vineyard of Naboth which her husband coveted.

18:17, 18). It may be wondered why Ahab bothered to speak to him at all, instead of having him arrested and executed, as he had no doubt intended. It is evident, however, that Ahab was in a state of desperation over the continued drought. Crops had failed, the people were starving, cattle and flocks were dying. The man who had warned him that this would happen was this bedraggled, but awesome, holy preacher, and it is true that thereafter he had sought to punish this messenger of doom and vehement denouncer of idolatry. But Ahab was clearly indifferent on the subject of religion; and although he had done nothing to stop his wife's paganism, had allowed her to retain the priests of her deities and had not countered her death sentences on the Hebrew priests, he was no Baal missionary. As to his attitude towards the faith of Israel, it was lack of concern rather than outright hostility — after all, he retained Obadiah as master of his household though he must have known the private religious views of this official. Now, hearing Elijah speak, and being utterly at a loss as to what to do about the drought, he may have thought

that the messenger of doom might yet prove to be a messenger of hope.

It was in this mood that he listened to and accepted the proposal now made by Elijah, whose principal purpose was to use the drought crisis as a pretext for a showdown with paganism and deal it a decisive blow. He told the king to arrange for a mass assembly on the top of Mount Carmel to witness a trial of strength between God, represented by Elijah himself, and Baal, who would be represented by the eight hundred and fifty priests who had been brought to the kingdom of Israel from Phoenicia.

CONTEST WITH BAAL

When all were assembled on Carmel, Elijah, addressing himself primarily to the ambivalent, cried out: "How long will you go limping with two different opinions? If the Lord is God, follow him; but if Baal, then follow him" (I Kings 18:21). He then proposed that all the pagan priests should choose a bull and place it on wood, and he, Elijah, would do the same, and "you call on the name of your god and I will call on the name of

89

Magnificent 9th century BC ivory plaques, some bearing inscriptions in ancient Hebrew script, were discovered at archaeological excavations at Samaria and are known as the "Samarian Ivories". Recording "the acts of Ahab", the Bible specifically mentions "the ivory house which he built". (1 Kings 22:39).

the Lord", and whichever divinity sent down fire to consume the sacrifice "he is God".

The contest began in the early morning, the priests praying to their deity; and when nothing happened, they leapt frenziedly round their altar, slashing themselves "with swords and lances" and calling on their Baal to respond to their entreaties. "But there was no voice; no one answered, no one heeded" (I Kings 18:29). The populace looked on in suspense, and Elijah with contempt. "Cry aloud", he mocked at the false prophets, "for he is a god; either he is musing, or he has gone aside, or he is on a journey, or perhaps he is asleep and must be awakened" (I Kings 18:27). The taunts goaded them to more furious ravings and mutilations, but to no avail. The day was nearing its end.

Then Elijah told the people to draw near. To show the magnitude of the Lord's power, he made the contest harder for his cause by drenching his altar with water. He then turned to heaven and cried: "Answer me, O Lord, answer me, that this people may know that Thou, O Lord, art God, and that Thou hast turned their hearts back". Suddenly, the altar

was enveloped in flames and all was consumed — even the water which had flowed into the surrounding trench. From the awe-struck assembly rose a great shout: "The Lord, he is God; the Lord, he is God" (I Kings 18:39). Elijah took quick advantage of the revolutionary impact on the people. "Seize the prophets of Baal", he roared at them, "let not one of them escape". And the pagan priests were dragged down to the brook of Kishon and killed.

Ahab had been a mute witness of these dramatic happenings, taking no steps to intervene. Elijah now came to tell him that he could hear "a sound of the rushing of rain". The drought was about to end. The prophet went up to the ridge of Carmel and sent his servant seven times to a lookout point to watch the sky over the sea. After the seventh time, the servant reported: "Behold, a little cloud like a man's hand is rising out of the sea" (I Kings 18:44). Elijah told him to tell Ahab to prepare his chariot and go home before the rains stopped him. Ahab did so, proceeding to his winter palace in the valley of Jezreel. The heavens suddenly grew black

with cloud and torrential rains followed.

It is indeed true that, with its long sweep seawards, the Carmel is the first of Israel's heights to meet the rains. It is an imposing range, covered with oak and carob and wild bush, and with a profusion of flowers in the spring, its ridges offering glorious prospects of the sea on the west, Jezreel on the east and the hills of Galilee on the north. This was the site chosen for the decisive battle of the spirit, with the triumph of Israel's faith and the rout of the invading paganism which had threatened to crush it.

"A STILL SMALL VOICE"

Elijah had played the key role of his prophetic life; but that life was now in danger. For Ahab had recounted the fantastic events to Jezebel as soon as he reached the palace and Jezebel vowed to have Elijah slain, as her priests had been slain, within twenty four hours. The prophet promptly fled, heading south to Beersheba, where he left his servant and proceeded alone into the desert of Sinai. After a day and night of depression and exhaustion — and doubt whether he was

Ba'al in the house of Ba'al which made an Asherah *(1 Kings 16:32, 33)*

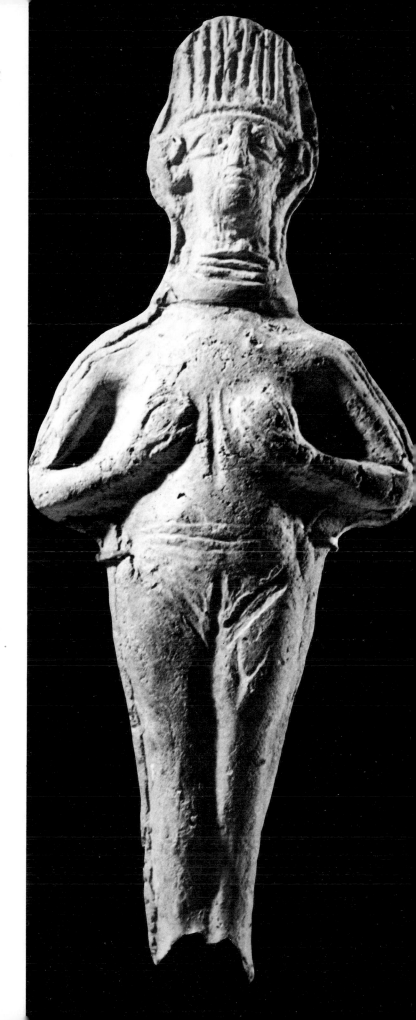

Phoenician princess Jezebel brought images of gods
and goddesses from her native Sidon to Israel
upon her marriage to king Ahab. Her attempts
to impose paganism upon court and country
met with powerful resistance, led by the prophet Elijah.

doing any good by going on living in a world
of so much wickedness — he was touched
by an angel and miraculously provided with
food. He then roused himself to make a forty
day pilgrimage to Mount Horeb, where Moses
had received the Ten Commandments. Here,
at the source of the Hebrew faith, where the
Covenant had been consummated between
God and the Israelites, Elijah sought to re-
fresh his spirit and find a renewal of the
word of God in a personal revelation. From
the biblical record of Elijah's divine encounter, we discover a vital nuance which was to
have a lasting impact on the Jewish religion.

He ascended the craggy slopes to the peak
of Sinai to meet the divine presence, and a
wind suddenly rose of such violence that it
seemed to split the rock; "but the Lord was
not in the wind". Then came an earthquake;
"but the Lord was not in the earthquake".
It was followed by fire; "but the Lord was
not in the fire". But after the fire there came
"a still small voice. And when Elijah heard
it, he wrapped his face in his mantle" (I Kings
19:11–13). It was this "still small voice",
the voice of the Lord, that was the spiritual

Elijah resuscitating the child of
the widow, portrayed in the wall painting
from the synagogue of Dura-Europos.

essence of religion, not the external phenom-
ena of the elements, which were themselves
subject to the power of God. This spiritual
aspect had always been there, since the time
of Moses; but it had been latent. Henceforth
it would be "increasingly stressed", as the
renowned scholar William Foxwell Albright
points out, "and the external character of His
theophany in nature was more and more re-
stricted to the sphere of poetic imagery".

From Sinai Elijah proceeded on divine instructions to Damascus — on a revolutionary
political mission which presaged the eventual
overthrow of the house of Omri and Ahab —
and on the way back, passing through the
Jordan valley, he met a young man, Elisha,
at Abel-Meholah where he was ploughing his
father's land. The youth left plough and family and followed Elijah for the rest of the
prophet's life.

NABOTH'S VINEYARD

The outstanding episode where Elijah is revealed as the champion of justice, bitterly
denouncing the wickedness not only of man
to God but also of man to man, even when

of Elijah; and the soul of the child came into him again, and he revived

(1 Kings 17:22)

The landscape of Gilead on the east bank of the river Jordan, birthplace of Elijah.

the offender is the king himself, was the cruel acquisition of Naboth's vineyard, which is recounted in I Kings 21. Ahab wanted a vineyard which adjoined his royal estate in Jezreel, but the owner, Naboth, refused to part with "the inheritance of my fathers". Jezebel, remembering the unlimited powers of the Phoenician court where she had been raised, was incensed that her husband, the king of Israel, could not get what he wanted. She accordingly arranged for "two base fellows" to bring a public charge of blasphemy against Naboth, who was arraigned and stoned to death. His property then reverted to the Crown, and Ahab took it without a murmur against his wife's action.

When the news reached Elijah, he rushed in fury to the palace and hurled at Ahab the fierce reproach: "Haratzachta vegan yarashta?" — so much more powerful in the original Hebrew than in its translation: "Have you killed, and also taken possession?" He then predicted the doom of the dynasty: as for Ahab himself, "In the place where dogs licked up the blood of Naboth shall dogs lick your own blood"; and as for his wife, "The dogs

Elijah abode for a time in "the upper chamber" of a house in a northern village, and it was there that he performed the miracle of restoration.

shall eat Jezebel within the bounds of Jezreel". For the first time we find Ahab reacting with humility, rending his clothes, donning sackcloth and fasting. Such signs of repentance brought him a deferment of Elijah's curse.

Elijah's end is a sudden and eerie as his first appearance. Feeling that death was near, he went from Gilgal to Bethel and on to Jericho — all three were centres of prophetic groups — accompanied by his disciple Elisha, and on they strode eastwards to the river Jordan, which they crossed. They went on walking and talking when suddenly "a chariot of fire and horses of fire separated the two of them. And Elijah went up by a whirlwind into heaven" (II Kings 2:11).

THE WONDERS OF ELISHA

Elisha was markedly different in personality from his teacher, gentle (though he could be firm when necessary) where his teacher was stern and forceful, gregarious where Elijah was solitary. But he was equally unswerving in his condemnation of the moral laxity of

As Elijah sent word to Ahab of the imminent advent of rain after the prolonged drought, clouds came up over the sea and darkened the skies above Carmel.

his times and equally fervent in his cause of
the Lord.

He is presented in the Bible as pursuing
his mission through the working of miracles.
The waters of the principal spring of Jericho
have become foul and he makes them wholesome (II Kings 2:19–22). (The spring of
Ain-es-Sultan is traditionally known as the
"Spring of Elisha", and its gushing waters
still bestow luxuriance upon the Jericho
area.) Like his predecessor, he multiplies the
quantity of a single jar of oil (II Kings
4:1–7). Also like Elijah, he restores life to
a dead child (II Kings 4:21–37). When there
is a famine, he turns poisonous wild gourds
into a palatable meal (II Kings 4:38–44).
He cures the leprosy of the Aramaean general,
Na'aman (II Kings 5). And there are other
beneficent wonders attributed to Elisha —
though one, uncharacteristically, was hardly
beneficent. This was his summoning of two
she-bears who came out of the woods and
mauled some young boys who had jeered and
called him "baldhead" (II Kings 2:23, 24).

Elisha, too, had dealings with the king of
Israel, and he could be as censorious as

Sheepskin coats popular in Israel today recall the kind of garment worn by the prophet Elijah, as suggested in the biblical description of his encounter with the messengers of king Ahaziah of Israel.

Elijah; but he made no dramatic entrances into the royal tent or palace, and the meetings were not at his but at the royal initiative. The principal difference, however, was that while Elijah was always opposed to the king, Elisha was usually helpful, though admittedly on occasion reluctantly so. The times had changed and so had the kings. Ahab was dead, killed in battle at Ramoth-Gilead, and his body was brought back in his chariot for burial in Samaria. "And they washed the chariot by the pool of Samaria, and the dogs licked up his blood" (I Kings 22:38), as Elijah had predicted. After the brief reign of his son Ahaziah, another son, Jehoram, ascended the throne, and though his mother Jezebel was still alive, paganism was less dominant than it had been in Ahab's day. This was due largely to the achievements of Elijah, and the anti-Baal forces, encouraged by him, had become increasingly strong. Jehoram was sensitive to this change, and though he introduced no major religious reform, he at least "put away the pillar of Baal which his father had made" (II Kings 3:2). Elisha could thus cooperate with him more than

Elijah could have done with king Ahab.

Moreover, the danger of foreign invasion was now greater, and in such moments the pious were patriotic. Indeed, the priests and "the sons of the prophets" (II Kings 6:1) were among the most ardent patriots, and when the country was threatened, they would accompany the troops in the field. Elisha did too, and he would certainly help the king and the army to overcome the enemy. (Incidentally, the "sons of the prophets" were groups of pious men who lived with their families on the communal pattern, dedicated to God, and, like Elijah, wore "a garment of hair cloth, with a girdle of leather about [their] loins" [II Kings 1:8]. Elisha often lived in such communes, for the most part with the ones in the vicinity of Gilgal in the Jericho plain.) However, their loyalty was to the country and to their faith, based as it was on the Covenant with God, and whenever they felt that this Covenant was being ignored or abrogated by the king, they did not fail to criticize him, and even — as Elisha eventually did with Jehoram — take revolutionary action against him.

A ROYAL MEETING

We are told of Elisha's first royal meeting when Jehoram of Israel was joined by Jehoshaphat of Judah in a campaign against Moab. They decided to surprise the Moabites from the rear by following a circuitous route through the wilderness of Edom (whose king was their ally), and they ran out of water. Jehoshaphat asked whether there was not a prophet of the Lord who could help them, and someone said that Elisha was with the troops. The two kings went out to see him and explained their problem. Elisha's first reaction was to turn to Jehoram with the words: "What have I to do with you? Go to the prophets of your father and the prophets of your mother" (II Kings 3:13). For he could not pass over in silence the king's toleration of Jezebel's deities and her influence, however weakened. And though he was of course determined to save the army, he did not wish to appear to be acceding to a request from a not too repentant son of a pagan. He therefore went on to say that he agreed to help only out of respect for the virtuous Judean king: "were it not that I have regard

behold, a chariot of fire and horses of fire... And Elijah went up by a whirlwind into heaven (II Kings 2:11)

Sartaba, a hilltop overlooking the river Jordan, is popularly believed to be the spot where Elijah rose heavenwards in a fiery chariot. The ruins are those of a fortress built by the Hasmonean king Alexander Jannaeus and named Alexandrion. In Talmudic times it was one of the chain of hills on which beacons were lit to announce the new moon.

for Jehoshaphat the king of Judah, I would neither look at you, nor see you". He then made a hopeful prediction, and next morning, what had been a dry wadi was filled with water, and men and animals could slake their thirst. (Flash floods are not uncommon in the region.) Furthermore, the dawn sun on the surface of the water — an unusual sight during the dry season — gave it the colour of blood, and the enemy troops thought the allies had had a falling out and slaughtered each other. They made an undisciplined rush to the Hebrew camp to grab booty, and were cut to pieces.

Later, when the Aramaeans were invading Israel, Elisha's intelligence of the enemy's movements, which he passed on to the king, helped to save the country. Whether by supernatural powers or through information received from the groups of prophets who may thus have served as an intelligence network, Elisha seemed to know where the Aramaean king established his headquarters and the places he planned to attack, and he passed the news to the Israel troops who took appropriate action. They were apparently so

Wadi Kelt, near Jericho, where groups of
pious men in the time of Elisha dwelt in
isolated communes. The tradition was followed
one and a half millennia later by
the early Christians.

effective that the enemy king thought there must be a spy among his own people. But an aide told him that it was "Elisha, the prophet . . . who tells the king of Israel the words that you speak in your bedchamber" (II Kings 6:12). Elisha at that time was in Dothan, some ten miles north of Samaria, and an Aramaean unit was sent to capture him. Elisha entreated the Lord and his would-be captors were stricken with blindness. The prophet then went to them, posed as a guide and promised to lead them to the man they sought. He then led them right into Samaria where he turned them over to the king, who wanted to slay them. But Elisha advised clemency, and they were fed and allowed to return unharmed to their headquarters. This wise political act gained a respite for the Israelites.

Later still, when the Aramaeans again invaded Israel, they penetrated as far as Samaria, the capital, and put it under siege. The people in the city starved, and the king blamed their plight on Elisha, who had been telling them to have trust in the Lord. At the critical moment, when the situation was desperate and the city close to capitulation, the besieging forces suddenly vanished. Through Elisha's intervention, the Lord had caused them to hear the sounds of a great army coming up against them. In their bewilderment over the imagined commotion, they thought it was a host of Anatolian and Egyptian troops who, presumably, had come to join in an alliance with Israel. Fearing themselves outnumbered, they had fled in panic.

As we have seen, so long as Jehoram was on the throne and the land in danger, Elisha and his pious followers supported him against the invader. But at no time was there any let-up in their criticism of the domestic policies of the king. He was no leader in the Covenant tradition and no firm upholder of the Covenant laws. On the contrary, he had not stamped out the imported cult of paganism — his mother Jezebel was free and active — and he and his privileged establishment were tempted more by the laxness, decadence and luxury of a Phoenician court than by the stern, austere and moral principles expected of Israel's leaders. Some of the prophetic criticism found its influence in the

Now the men of the city (Jericho) said to Elisha, 'Behold... the water is bad... Then he went to the spring of water and threw salt in it (11 Kings 2:19, 21)

The Spring of Elisha in Jericho (left), whose foul waters were made wholesome by the prophet who inherited the mantle of Elijah.
The archaeological mound of Dothan (below), to the north of Samaria, where Elisha's would-be captors were struck blind.

army ranks, and this, coupled with their dissatisfaction over the ineffective way in which the war with the Aramaeans was being waged — Jehoram was clearly no Saul or David — aroused a revolutionary ferment among the commanders. It was encouraged by Elisha, whose commitment was not to "king and country" but to "country and faith", and if there was a chance of replacing Jehoram, he was all in favor of seizing it. At the height of a campaign when Israel was encamped against the Aramaeans at Ramoth-Gilead, taking advantage of the king's incapacity — he had been wounded — one of the Israel generals, Jehu, spurred by Elisha, led a successful army revolt and coup d'etat. Jehoram and his mother were slain and the dynasty of Omri and Ahab was wiped out, in fulfillment of Elijah's prophecy. The "harlotries and the sorceries" of Jezebel were abolished, the pagan temples destroyed, their priests and worshippers put to death, and the cult of Baal and Asherah was eradicated.

The two 9th century BC prophets, notably Elijah, are among the most colorful and dramatic of the biblical seers. They fight as

soldiers of the Lord against pagan worship, berate the king, champion the downtrodden and contribute in a unique way to the moral development of the nation in this early period of the divided monarchy. In their personalities, they were strange prophets, unlike any who came before or after. Neither could claim the statesmanlike qualities of their predecessors. Statesmanship was not their style. Nor was either of them possessed of the poetic genius of their successors — though there were times when Elijah used words in a manner equalled by the greatest of the biblical stylists. Both breathed fire and were volcanoes of fanaticism, and that was just what was required at that period to jerk the people out of their ambivalence and complacency.

Elijah remains to this day one of the great folk heroes of the nation, and he, perhaps more than any other Old Testament seer, still keeps a lively hold on the public mind — he is even the subject of popular songs sung in modern Israel. In Jewish tradition, Elijah continues to wander the earth, to reappear as the forerunner of the Messiah and the redemption of man. The tradition is long, and

was presumably strong even in biblical times, for his re-appearance is indicated in the scriptures, as we see from the 6th century BC prophet Malachi: "Behold, I will send you Elijah the prophet before the great and terrible day of the Lord comes" (4:5). Today, at the Passover *seder* celebrated by Jews throughout the world, an extra cup of wine is poured for Elijah and the door is opened in case he should walk in.

5. THE VISIONARY GENIUS

When the war-weary men of our own generation established the United Nations Organization, they could find no words more appropriate to express its aims and inscribe on a stone wall near the entrance to its building in New York than the visionary view of the ideal world uttered by a Jew of Jerusalem more than two and a half millennia earlier: "And they shall beat their swords into ploughshares, and their spears into pruning hooks; nation shall not lift up sword against nation, neither shall they learn war any more" (Isa. 2:4).

The man was Isaiah, after Moses the greatest of the Hebrew prophets, inspired and inspiring seer, mighty reservoir of spiritual force, intellectual giant and practical statesman, who set forth his vast wisdom in poetic Hebrew of unmatched power, beauty and impact. Isaiah towers over the 8th century BC — and over all the centuries thereafter.

The 8th was indeed a century in sore need of a commanding guide. It was a century of tragedy which witnessed the fall of the northern kingdom of Israel (in 722 BC); and this was the forerunner of the calamity which would overtake the southern kingdom of Judah 135 years later. The latter part of the 8th century thus marked a turning point in the fortunes of the Hebrew nation. As a consequence, it produced a fundamental change in the character of the prophets and in the nature of their utterances.

Up to then, seeking to strengthen the religious and ethical fibre of the people, the prophets had often made gloomy predictions of what would happen if there were a continued departure from the standards which had been set by the Covenant; but none had envisaged the total destruction of the kingdoms. The Lord would punish infractions — a king would be dethroned; the land would suffer drought; an enemy attack might succeed and territory would be lost. But in times of grave emergency, the Lord would somehow save the day. He would not allow the nation to go under.

This attitude had been largely conditioned by the political and military conjunture which had prevailed in the Middle East for the previous five hundred years. Between the 13th and the 8th centuries BC neither Egypt

and they shall beat their swords into ploughshares,
and their spears into pruning hooks;
nation shall not lift up sword against nation,
neither shall they learn war any more   (Isaiah 2:4)

The beautifully preserved Hebrew scroll of the complete
Book of Isaiah discovered in the Dead Sea caves and now
in the Israel Museum, Jerusalem. A key extract from
the visionary words of this ancient prophet adorns the
portals of the United Nations building in New York
to express the lofty aims of the world Organization.

I am no prophet, nor a prophet's son; but I am a herdsman, and a dresser of sycamore trees (Amos 7:14)

The fruit of the sycamore tree (left) and the tree itself (right). Amos disdained the prophetic title, insisting that he was a herdsman and a dresser of sycamore-figs, a man of the soil who happened to have received the divine call to prophesy to his people.

in the south nor any of the powers in the north had proved strong enough to make a vigorous imperial thrust or engage in an imperial clash which would bring both sides battling across the lands which lay between them. These lands could thus develop in their own way, advancing their welfare if their leaders were wise, retarding it if they were inept. They could of course fight among themselves — and they did, constantly. All experienced ups and downs, gaining or losing a battle, demanding or having to pay tribute; but none lived under the constant awesome fear of annihilation by an imperial giant. The emergence of the powerful, northern, Assyrian empire shortly after the middle of the 8th century put an end to that epoch. The danger of total destruction was now very real to Aram, Ammon, Moab, Edom, Phoenicia, Philistia — and to the kingdoms of Israel and Judah.

This posed vastly new problems to the keepers of the national conscience, for their teaching and guidance had now to take account of the possibility that statehood and independence might be lost. The extraordi-

The rocky site of ancient Tekoa,
birthplace of the prophet **Amos**,
at the edge of the wilderness of **Judea**.

nary way in which they and their successors rose to the challenge may not always have saved their own generations; but it ensured the national and spiritual preservation of the Hebrew people for all time.

Thus, if Elijah and Elisha, formidable as they were, were more folk figures whose legends lasted but whose influence was largely limited to the age and area in which they lived, the impact of the prophets who came after them, notably Isaiah and, later, Jeremiah, was immense and boundless, extending long beyond their own age and even beyond the frontiers of their own nation.

THE LITERARY PROPHETS

Apart from Isaiah, there were three notable prophets in the 8th century. The first were Amos and Hosea, and these two started the new prophetic trend. Amos, first of the "literary" prophets, "was among the shepherds of Tekoa", a village at the edge of the Judean wilderness, though he prophesied in the northern kingdom, and he started his public life towards the end of the reigns of Uzziah king of Judah and Jeroboam II of Israel. Hosea,

Inscription marking the final resting place of
"the bones of Uzziah king of Judah", who had contracted
leprosy and had therefore not been buried in the royal tombs.

who came from the northern kingdom, was active there at about the same time. The third prophet was Micah. He was born in Moresheth, in the foothills facing the Mediterranean coastal plain in southwestern Judah, and his utterances, contemporary with those of Isaiah, started a little later, during the reigns of Jotham, Ahaz and Hezekiah, king of Judah.

The moral collapse of the northern kingdom began with the death of Jeroboam II in 745 BC, and it led to political anarchy which ended with the end of the State. During those last disastrous twenty-four years, the scene in Samaria was marked by plot and counterplot, seizure of the throne by violence, usurper overthrown by usurper in civil war, the breakdown of law and order, and an upsurge in irreligious and licentious behaviour. All this went on while the inexorable tread of the invader moved steadily closer.

Judah, too, though more stable politically and somewhat less errant in its religious ways, was nevertheless lax, wanton and indecisive during this period, and seemed also to be floundering amid the alarming portents of

Jerusalem, the view from the southwest. The gilded Dome of the Rock (upper left). located on the original site of Solomon's Temple, and the silver-domed Mosque of El-Aksa, to its right, stand within the enclosure of the ancient Jewish Temple Mount. Above it, the Hebrew University buildings on the ridge of Mount Scopus. The Western Wall, Jewry's most sacred site, appears below and left of the golden dome.

The prophet Isaiah, from the frescoes
by Michelangelo in the Vatican's Sistine chapel
painted at the beginning of the 16th century.

Assyrian moves. Lying further south, it was less immediately vulnerable; but the threat was still real. Yet its leaders spent more time searching for diplomatic alliances of dubious expediency than in gearing the people to meet the growing peril.

The three prophets of humble origin had no personal dealings with kings and courts, nor with the official priesthood, whom they despised. They were not men of action and are credited with no miracles. They were men of words, inspired words, and of courage. They roamed the countryside, speaking out fearlessly in the market-place, as well as in the Temple courts, teaching, guiding, appealing to the conscience of the people and entreating them to keep their Covenant with the Lord. Of course, like earlier prophets, they railed against idolatry and immorality and against the greed, hypocrisy and abuse of power by the authorities. They also denounced the social evils, notably the dishonesty of the rich and the exploitation of the poor. More significant, however, and quite a new prophetic feature, was their attack on the religious establishment. They deplored the preoccupation with the external rituals and urged that faith was a matter of the heart and the conscience. "For I desire steadfast love and not sacrifice, the knowledge of God, rather than burnt offerings", cries Hosea (6:6). And Micah says: "Will the Lord be pleased with thousands of rams, with ten thousands of rivers of oil? . . . what does the Lord require of you but to do justice, and to love kindness, and to walk humbly with your God?" (6:7, 8). This novel note in the prophetic strain was to be echoed by all who followed them — and was to prove a powerful bulwark in sustaining the nation when it was thrust into exile, and in preserving its religion even though bereft of the Temple. For Temple worship and Temple sacrifice were not essential to religion. The heart of the faith was faith in the heart.

The core of the good society was justice. Amos had a vision of the Lord with a plumb line in his hand standing beside a wall and saying: "Behold, I am setting a plumb line in the midst of my people Israel; I will never again pass by them; the high places of Isaac shall be made desolate, and the sanctuaries

this iniquity shall be to you like a break in a high wall, bulging out, and about to collapse (Isaiah 30:13)

Ruined walls in Sebaste, on the site of the earlier Samaria whose destruction, because of its iniquity, was foretold by Isaiah. It was like a flawed wall, he said, "whose crash comes suddenly".

of Israel shall be laid waste" (Amos 7:8, 9). Professor Shalom Spiegel writes: "It is a homely lesson any mason could understand and impart: a wall to stand and to endure must be straight and strong, without fault of construction. If it be out of plumb, the taller the wall, the surer its fall. The imagery seems to suggest that what the law of gravitation is to nature, justice is to society".

However, the most striking aspect of the teachings of Amos and Hosea, which launched a new tradition, was their courageous acceptance, and presentation, of the awesome implications of the basic principle inherent in the Mosaic Covenant. If the people abandoned the stipulations of that covenant, they would in turn be abandoned by the Lord. Unless they changed their evil ways and repented, they would be judged — in the harshest possible terms. If they thought that they could never be torn from God's Promised Land, and that some charismatic Judge or a miracle-working prophet would arise to save them, they were grievously mistaken. Amos and Hosea were there to tell them that they might not be saved. The Lord would no

longer be committed to his promise — even of the land — if they disregarded their own obligations undertaken at Sinai. It was therefore fruitless for them to go on in their old ways and look for mighty deeds of rescue. They should look into their own hearts, and alter their behavior, seek the hard road to understanding rather than the mythical track to easy rescue, otherwise the only mighty deeds they could expect would be acts of divine punishment.

Here, then, were prophets who were offering not comfort, not miracles, but warnings of doom. Some of those who followed in the next three centuries were, like Hosea with his "they sow the wind, and they shall reap the whirlwind" (8:7), fierce prophets of disaster. Some were prophets of pure hope. But all, even Hosea and Jeremiah, were unable to suppress the note of hopeful promise which was cardinal to the Hebrew faith, with visions of idyllic happiness once there was a reconciliation with the Lord.

If the utterances of these prophets had so profound an effect on later generations, not least of the reasons was the sublime poetry

An Assyrian relief in the palace of Sennacherib at Nineveh shows captives being driven out of their destroyed city and spoil being carried off by the conquering troops. Imperialism and the glorification of imperialist exploits roused the prophet Isaiah to bitter denunciation.

with which they expressed their sublime thoughts, rich in picturesque simile, using words as they had never been used before, and, for their imagery, drawing upon familiar scenes from life around them, easily understandable by the ordinary man.

ISAIAH'S "FAITHFUL CITY"

In no individual were the genius of thought and the genius of expression more happily blended than in Isaiah the son of Amoz. Yet unlike the other prophets of that or any century, he combined these gifts with other qualities of understanding and personality which gave his voice an honored hearing — not always followed — in the councils of state. He was thus able to some extent to influence the practical course of current affairs as well as making an indelible mark on the future of his people.

He was born in Jerusalem close to the middle of the 8th century BC and his entire life was bound up with this "faithful city" as he called it. This was Zion, the city of David, with its Temple Mount and the valley of Kidron and the slopes of Olives and Scopus

The Black Obelisk of the Assyrian emperor Shalmaneser III recording his military conquests and depicting his vassals bringing rich tribute and humbling themselves before him.

set amid the surroundings of the Judean hills. It was a city of ineluctable beauty and historic glory, the spiritual centre of the nation, the city whose every stone was dear to him — and the city which he castigated because he loved. It was natural that in his vision of the ideal world, the source of inspiration of that world would be the place from which he had drawn his own: "It shall come to pass in the latter days that the mountain of the house of the Lord shall be established as the highest of the mountains, and shall be raised above the hills; and all the nations shall flow to it, and many peoples shall come, and say: 'Come let us go up to the mountain of the Lord, to the house of the God of Jacob; that He may teach us His ways and that we may walk in His paths'. For out of Zion shall go forth the law, and the word of the Lord from Jerusalem" (Isa. 2:2, 3).

[Professor Moshe Weinfeld of the Hebrew University, Jerusalem, points out that the Jerusalem Temple served as a high court for the country. It was there that the people received instruction and from there came the verdict or the final decision. The details are to be found in Deuteronomy 17:8 ff, and there the Hebrew word "Torah" (Deut. 17:11), commonly signifying "the Law", is used as "instructions", and the Hebrew word "davar" (Deut. 17:8 and 10), which also means "word", is used in the sense of "decision". Thus, Isaiah's vision of the ideal world saw the Temple as an international court giving forth "instruction" to the peoples of all countries, and issuing "decisions" to settle international strife — the very first notion of an ideal United Nations Assembly. Using the Deuteronomy sense of "torah" and "davar", it was Isaiah's hope that "out of Zion shall go forth the *instruction,* and the *verdict* of the Lord from Jerusalem. Jerusalem, then, was a real and national court, and Isaiah, in his vision, as Dr. Weinfeld indicates, was converting it into an international spiritual court.]

Isaiah was in his early twenties when he received the prophetic call. This was in the latter part of the reign of king Uzziah, and for the next fifty years his was the dominant voice in the nation — mostly the voice of opposition. He had one major encounter with king Ahaz; but it is during the reign of king Hezekiah that Isaiah also comes into his own as a man of affairs.

By then his reputation had been well established. As a young man he witnessed the venality of the northern kingdom and watched it crumbling. When he looked around him in Jerusalem he saw similar signs of depravity and corruption, and he trembled at the likely consequences. He was alarmed at the equanimity of the people who shut their eyes to reality and their ears to the voice of correction, seeking only sweet words of reassurance: "For they are a rebellious people, lying sons, sons who will not hear the instruction of the Lord; who say to the seers, 'See not'; and to the prophets, 'Prophesy not to us what is right; speak to us smooth things, prophesy illusions'" (Isa. 30:9, 10). Isaiah's aim was to disillusion them. Embellishing Amos' parable of the wall and the plumb line, he said: "this iniquity shall be to you like a break in a high wall, bulging out, and about to collapse, whose crash comes suddenly, in an instant; and it smashes so ruthlessly . . ." (Isa. 30:13, 14). Iniquity in society was like a

the steep ravines... the clefts of the rocks... the thornbushes

(Isaiah 7:19)

The Judean wilderness. Isaiah drew upon
the landscape of the region for the symbolism
in his prophetic pronouncements.

structural crack which could bring the whole edifice crashing to the ground.

Also in the Amos tradition, Isaiah cried out: "Ah sinful nation, a people laden with iniquity, offspring of evildoers, sons who deal corruptly. They have forsaken the Lord ... How the faithful city has become a harlot, she that was full of justice ... Every one loves a bribe and runs after gifts ... Therefore the Lord says ... I will turn my hand against you and will smelt your dross ..." But a purified remnant would be left after this refining process, and "Zion shall be redeemed by justice, and those in her who repent, by righteousness" (Isa. 1:4, 21–27).

In the tradition of Hosea, he has these words for the priestly establishment and its hypocrisy: "What to me is the multitude of your sacrifices? says the Lord; I have had enough of burnt offerings of rams and the fat of fed beasts; I do not delight in the blood of bulls, or of lambs, or of he-goats ... Bring me no more vain offerings ..." What the Lord sought of the people was simply that they should "cease to do evil, learn to do good; seek justice, correct oppression; defend the fatherless, plead for the widow" (Isa. 1:11, 13, 16, 17). Each harangue includes constructive directions as to how the ills can be cured, and each ends with hope. Typical is: "Come now, let us reason together, says the Lord; though your sins are like scarlet, they shall be as white as snow; though they are red like crimson, they shall become like wool" (Isa. 1:18). The unrepentant would suffer, and there might be wide-scale destruction, but the nation would not be wiped out. "The light of Israel" would not be extinguished. It would "become a fire, and his Holy One a flame", kept ablaze by "the remnant of Israel and the survivors of the house of Jacob [who] will no more lean upon him that smote them, but will lean upon the Lord, the Holy One of Israel, in truth. A remnant will return, the remnant of Jacob, to the mighty God" (Isa. 10:17, 20, 21).

COUNSELLOR OF STATE
This faith in the Lord, this passionate sense of justice, and this hope of redemption through righteous behavior were integral to the spirit of Isaiah and they informed all his

Samaritan priest with a Torah scroll. The Samaritans are an ancient sect whose forebears were brought to Samaria by the Assyrians after their conquest of the northern kingdom of Israel in the 8th century BC and who later adopted a form of Judaism in which the Five Books of Moses (the Torah) alone were accepted as sacred scripture.

political concepts and his counsel to the head of state. We first come across his political advice at a meeting with the king which took place in the critical year 735. Pekah, on the throne of the northern kingdom, had formed an alliance with king Rezin of Damascus-Aram to march against the Assyrians. Presumably to secure their southern frontier, they invaded Judah, and soon their troops were almost at the gates of Jerusalem. The city was in a panic — and so was king Ahaz. Thinking himself helpless, he decided to appeal to the Assyrian emperor, Tiglath-Pileser III, for help. It was at this point that Isaiah had a confrontation with him. The prophet was full of confidence and sought to calm the king, allay his terror, straighten his spine. "Take heed, be quiet, do not fear", he said, "and do not let your heart be faint because of these two smouldering stumps of firebrands, at the fierce anger of Rezin and . . . the son of Remaliah [Pekah]" (Isa. 7:4). He urged the king to trust in the Lord — the attack by the Irael-Aram confederacy would not succeed, and there was no need to seek Assyrian aid. But the king had too little faith in the Lord, in himself and in his people. He ignored Isaiah's advice and sent huge gifts to the Assyrian emperor.

Tiglath-Pileser's reaction was swift. He thundered down upon the lands of the confederacy and overran them. He executed Rezin in 732 and would have done the same with Pekah if he had not been assassinated by Hoshea, who took the throne, promptly surrendered and put himself in tribute to the Assyrians. He was left as king of a much contracted Israel. Tiglath-Pileser died in 727 and was succeeded by his son Shalmaneser V. Hoshea seized the occasion to defect. Relying on promised help from the southern power, Egypt, he withheld his tribute to Assyria. In 724 Shalmaneser struck — and no help came from Egypt. Hoshea was taken prisoner and Samaria put under siege. The city held out for two years, during which time Shalmaneser died and was succeeded by Sargon II. In 722, Samaria fell, and the country was absorbed within the Assyrian empire. Of the surviving Israelites, many were deported to Mesopotamia; a large number fled southwards into Judah, rejoining their brothers; and some re-

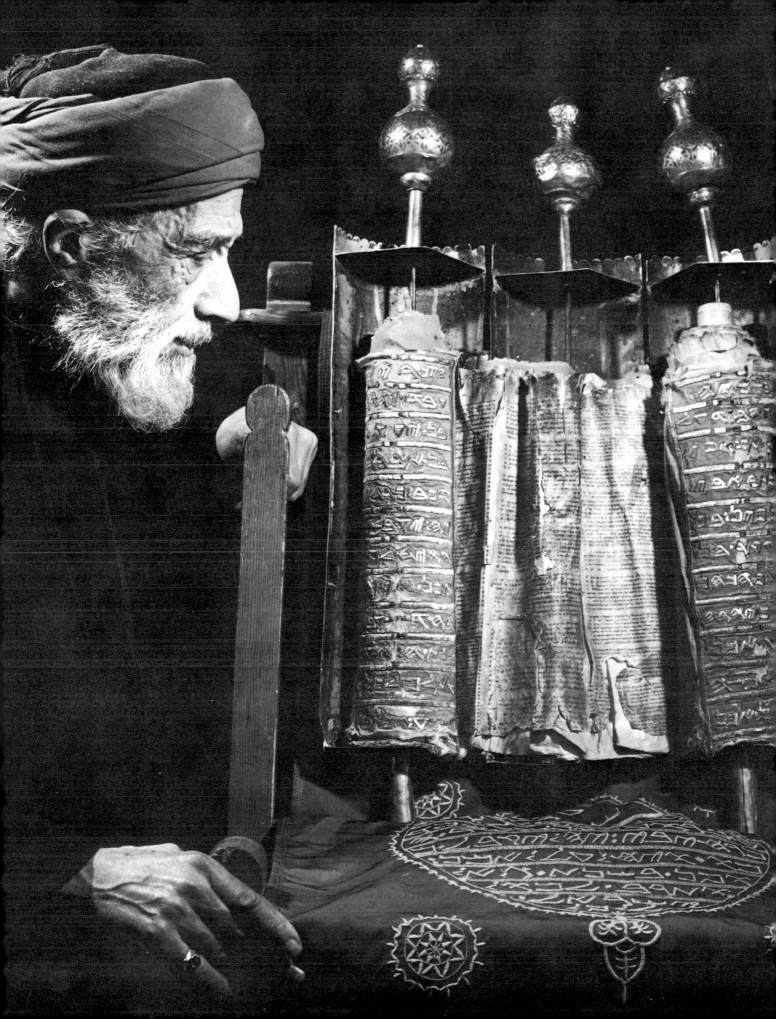

For the vineyard of the Lord of hosts is the house of Israel (Isaiah 5:7)

Wheatfields where "the harvestman gathereth
corn" (left) and vineyards where they
"gleaned grapes" (below), illustrative of scenes which
found poetic expression in Isaiah's prophecies.

mained. Sargon then peopled the territory with deportees from other lands which he had conquered, including "Babylon, Cuthah . . . [and] Hamath", and these people "took possession of Samaria, and dwelt in its cities" (II Kings 17:24). (The Israelites who had remained would assimilate with these northern deportees, and their descendants would be known as Samaritans, i.e. from Samaria.)

Judah had been given a respite — though she was in tribute to Assyria — and was now the only remnant of the nation in its own land. Jerusalem was now the sole national capital, home of the central sanctuary and trustee of the people's hopes. The responsibility was terrifying — and so was the shock of Israel's destruction and the enlarged power of the Assyrian empire, with its troops right on the Judean border. Isaiah was also shocked. He saw Israel's fate as the natural consequence of its behavior, and he knew that his task was to make Judah learn the lesson in time. Though he felt in his bones that the Lord would not allow Jerusalem to suffer the fate of Samaria, his head told him that this was possible if the corruption, indiffer-

ence and social injustice he saw all round him were not crushed.

PROPHETIC IMAGERY
The prophet went to the people with words of measureless worth on his lips, seeking to rouse them from their equanimity and rally their spiritual forces, and he was to do this for the rest of his life. In his moral precepts and his prophetic pronouncements, Isaiah drew upon the landscape of the region and the common scenes he encountered inside the city of Jerusalem as he walked its alleys and watched from his housetop. And so we read of the Judean hills, with their "desolate valleys" and "caves of the rocks" — much as they are today — and the fruitfulness, as now, of the wheatfields where "the harvestman gathereth corn" and the vineyards where they "gleaned grapes" and the groves where they "shook the olive tree". We get a vibrant picture of life inside Jerusalem with the crowds in the Temple courts and the milling multitudes in the narrow lanes, the horses and chariots, the "tumult" and the "movement" there. And we feel the prophet's out-

rage over the lust for material riches, for silver and gold, and the indulgence in "strong drink" and coarse festivities.

Amos and Hosea were of humble birth. Isaiah was evidently from a distinguished family (some scholars suggest that it may even have been close to the court in view of the ease with which the prophet could approach the king); yet he was as outspoken as his prophetic colleagues in his criticism of the nobility and the rich. "Your princes are rebels and companions of thieves" (Isa. 1:23). They "have devoured the vineyard" and taken "the spoil of the poor" (Isa. 3:14). "What do you mean", he cried, "by crushing my people, by grinding the face of the poor?" (Isa. 3:15). He deplored the avarice of the men of property: "Woe to those who join house to house, who add field to field" (Isa. 5:8).

He tried to make the people look at themselves and see how futile and dangerous was their indifference to the enemy at the gates and the frivolity in their midst, and he has a biting, but most precise and colorful, passage in which he likens them to the ladies of fashion and warns them of what will happen if they persist in their quest for ephemeral pleasures and adornment:

"The Lord said: 'Because the daughters of Zion are haughty and walk with outstretched necks, glancing wantonly with their eyes, mincing along as they go, tinkling with their feet; the Lord will smite with a scab the heads of the daughters of Zion, and the Lord will lay bare their secret parts. In that day the Lord will take away the finery of the anklets, the headbands, and the crescents; the pendants, the bracelets, and the scarfs; the headdresses, the armlets, the sashes, the perfume boxes, and the amulets; the signet rings and nose rings; the festal robes, the mantles, the cloaks, and the handbags; the garments of gauze, the linen garments, the turbans, and the veils. Instead of perfume there will be rottenness; and instead of a girdle, a rope; and instead of well-set hair, baldness; and instead of a rich robe, a girding of sackcloth; instead of beauty, shame" (Isa. 3:16–24).

HEZEKIAH'S TUNNEL
Hezekiah, who had succeeded his father Ahaz, began casting about for anti-Assyrian alli-

Jewellery worn by the "haughty" and "wanton" women at the time of Isaiah, a fashion which the prophet likened to the frivolity of his people in his biting diatribe against materialism.

ances among the neighboring states, and encouraging their overtures. Isaiah scorned such diplomacy, calling for faith in the Lord rather than in pagan allies. He was only slightly less scornful about the fortifications built by Hezekiah to protect Jerusalem. He was of course practical enough to recognize the importance of military defence. But neither ramparts nor earthworks would prove effective if the nation were afflicted with moral sickness and lacked the support of the Lord. "You looked to the weapons", he called out one day to Hezekiah, "and you saw that the breaches of the city of David were many, and you collected the waters of the lower pool, and you counted the houses of Jerusalem, and you broke down the houses to fortify the wall. You made a reservoir between the two walls for the water of the· old pool. But you did not look to Him who did it . . ." (Isa. 22:8–11).

Isaiah's mention of the "reservoir" and the "lower pool" was a reference to a spectacular project which Hezekiah had undertaken, and which had its echo in an amazing discovery ninety-five years ago. Knowing that if Jeru-

135

the quarrymen hewed (the rock), each man toward his fellow, axe against axe *(The Siloam Inscription)*

salem were put under siege it would hold out only for as long as it had water, Hezekiah concerned himself with ensuring the city's supply, safeguarding access to its sources and denying them to the enemy. Before the discovery, it was known only from the biblical Books of Isaiah, Kings and Chronicles that he accordingly "made the pool and the conduit and brought water into the city" (II Kings 20:20). "This same Hezekiah closed the upper outlet of the waters of Gihon and directed them down to the west side of the city of David" (II Chr. 32:30). The spring of Gihon, at the foot of the eastern wall, was the main source of the city's water, and what the king did was to seal the Gihon cave from which the spring issued, thereby shielding it from the enemy, and at the same time cut a tunnel under the wall which led the water by gravity flow into a reservoir or pool inside the city. This was the pool of Siloam (or Shiloah).

The 600 yard "conduit" remained in an excellent state of preservation, and not far from the exit an inscription was brought to light in 1880 telling how the underground

Iron tools of the period discovered at archaeological excavations in Israel.

passage had been excavated. The language was classical Hebrew prose, and its contents, style and script showed unmistakably that it had been written in the reign of Hezekiah. Six lines alone remained, but these were enough to tell the story of how the tunnel had been dug by two teams of miners starting at opposite ends, working towards each other and meeting in the middle. And "when the tunnel was driven through", the Siloam Inscription, as it is now called, continues, "the quarrymen hewed (the rock), each man toward his fellow, axe against axe; and the water flowed from the spring toward the reservoir for 1,200 cubits, and the height of the rock above the head(s) of the quarrymen was 100 cubits". This marvel of 8th century BC engineering is one of the dramatic sights of modern Jerusalem.

THE HAUGHTY STEWARD

There was another fascinating discovery in the same area one hundred years ago which, after some ingenious and scholarly detective work carried out in the 1950s, cast vivid light on one of Isaiah's diatribes against the self-pampering rich and the vain and ostentatious nobility: "Thus says the Lord God of hosts, 'Come, go to this steward, to Shebna, who is over the household, and say to him: What have you to do here . . . that you have hewn here a tomb for yourself, you who hew a tomb on the height, and carve a habitation for yourself in the rock?'" (Isa. 22:15, 16).

In 1870, the French archaeologist Clermont-Ganneau discovered a rock-cut tomb in the village of Siloam on the eastern scarp of the Kidron valley about one hundred yards to the south of the Temple Mount. Above the door of the facade was a sunken panel with a three-line inscription in ancient Hebrew script. To the right of the door was another inscription of one line. Both inscriptions were badly damaged — they appeared to have been mutilated, the one-liner irretrievably, by a hammer. Writing about the larger inscription in 1899, the archaeologist said that "the only word I have been able to read with certainty is the word 'Bayit' [Hebrew for 'House']". Assuming that the inscription belonged to a funerary monument, since Siloam was the "great city of the dead", he wrote that he had "sometimes conceived that this might be the tomb of Shebna, or one of his colleagues, for I fancied that I could read in the larger inscription the complete title 'asher al ha'-bayit' — namely, 'steward over the House' — but it is well to be on guard against these too sanguine illusions".

Clermont-Ganneau died before he had been able to complete the necessary verifications. This was done eighty years after his discovery by Professor Nahman Avigad of Jerusalem's Hebrew University, and he was able to decipher almost the whole of the inscription. He published his results in 1953 and the translation reads, in part: "This is [the sepulchre of . . .] yahu who is over the house", and it carries the usual addition to keep away grave-robbers: "There is no silver and no gold here . . . Cursed be the man who will open this".

The problem of course was to solve the mystery of the missing letters of the word ending in "yahu" — the name of the owner. Avigad consulted with his colleague Professor Yigael Yadin and the two archaeologists concluded that the occupant of the tomb had indeed been Shebna. The Hebrew phrase used by Isaiah for the steward "who is over the household" is indeed "asher al ha'bayit", and there are seven instances in the Bible where this title is used to connote a royal comptroller. But none seemed, at first glance, an appropriate candidate for the truncated name in the inscription. Only one came close, with a name ending in "iah". This was Obadiah, who was in charge of Ahab's palace in Samaria; but he was buried in the northern kingdom, not in Jerusalem.

However, the archaeologists showed that Shebanyahu was probably the full name of Shebna — both in the Bible and on ancient Hebrew seals, numerous Hebrew names ending in "a", like Ezra, Acha, Avda, were pet names (hypocoristica) for Azaryahu, Achi-yahu, Avadyahu, and the name Shebna as well as Shebanya and Shebanyahu are found on some seals.

The passage in Isaiah is now brought to life. The prophet was furious at the very idea of the construction by this prominent court official during his lifetime of an ostentatious tomb (there are signs that it may have

The Siloam Inscription (below) describing in
classical Hebrew prose how Hezekiah's water tunnel
was quarried. It was discovered in 1880
in the tunnel beneath the valley (left)
which skirts today's village of Silwan.

been crowned by a pyramid) and at his effrontery in locating it not underground but on the hill of Siloam where it could be seen by all. Isaiah must have been angered afresh each time he walked along the Kidron valley and saw this monstrous "tomb on the height", the pretentious work of a flaunting functionary who should have been setting an example of sober modesty at that desperate time and concerning himself with the ills of State rather than with profligate excursions in self-aggrandizement.

One of the reasons why Hezekiah for the most part rejected Isaiah's political advice, however courteously he may have listened, was the political change that seemed to be overtaking the region in the early years of his reign. It held the promise of a change in the balance of forces, and the king was tempted by thoughts of shaking off Judah's tribute to Assyria and regaining full freedom. Sargon was heavily preoccupied with campaigns in the north — in Babylonia and Asia Minor. At the same time, internal weaknesses in Egypt had been exploited by a vigorous Ethiopian king, Piankhi, who overran the country,

turned it into a vassal state, and subsequently established the Twenty-fifth Ethiopian dynasty. There was now a southern power which seemed capable of competing with the northern power. The lands which lay between them, in tribute to Assyria, were thus courted by Egypt and encouraged to rebel against their northern master. Several towns in Philistia, notably Ashdod, responded to the blandishments of Ethiopian-dominated Egypt. Judah was also approached — envoys of the Ethiopian king actually came to Hezekiah's court to invite him to join the rebellion, promising him aid. This we know from chapter 18 of Isaiah as well as from Assyrian records which add that Edom and Moab were approached by Egypt with a similar offer.

Hezekiah was eager to accept. Isaiah railed against such a course, and took to "walking naked and barefoot" (Isa. 20:2) about Jerusalem to symbolize the fate of those foolish enough to trust Egypt. There were apparently others at court who sided with the prophet, and apparently Judah did not join the revolt. Ashdod and her neighboring towns did, in 713. Two years later they were dust and

Hezekiah... made the pool and the conduit and brought water into the city *(2 Kings 20:20)*

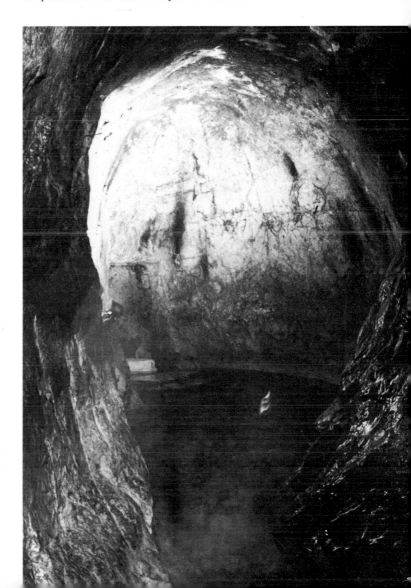

Interior of the Siloam tunnel, quarried at the time of Isaiah, which brought the waters from the Gihon spring by gravity flow to the pool inside the walled city of Jerusalem.

ashes. Assyria had struck in full force. Egypt had sent no aid to the rebels. (They even handed over to the Assyrians Ashdod's king who had escaped to Egypt.)

These events seem to have chastened Hezekiah, for we now find him very receptive to the religious appeals of Isaiah and of the contemporary prophet Micah, and introducing radical religious reforms. Over the next few years he repaired the Temple, purified and re-dedicated it, broke up the idols which had been tolerated in the previous reign and outlawed pagan worship. He sent couriers to the survivors of Israel to come to Jerusalem to join in the celebration of the Passover festival, thus symbolizing the restoration of Jerusalem as the national shrine of all the Israelites. In those years, too, as a result of the constant prodding of the two prophets, he removed the more glaring of the social evils and economic abuses in the state. Thus, in both Kings and Chronicles he is praised for his righteousness, and "the people took confidence from the words of Hezekiah king of Judah" (II Chr. 32:8).

What have you to do here... that you have hewn here a tomb for yourself... a tomb on the height, and carve a habitation for yourself in the rock? (Isaiah 22:16)

The funerary caves on the eastern scarp of the Kidron valley (left). This is the area where the haughty steward erected an ostentatious tomb for himself (below) in his lifetime, which so provoked the contempt and scorn of Isaiah.

PSYCHOLOGICAL WARFARE

However, Hezekiah's political outlook had not changed, and when the Assyrian emperor Sargon was killed in 705 BC and was succeeded by his son Sennacherib, who was promptly faced with rebellions by Babylon and Phoenicia, Hezekiah decided to break free by withholding Judah's tribute. While Sennacherib was thus engaged in the north, the lands to the south formed a rebel coalition, in which Judah was very active — Hezekiah event sent ambassadors to Egypt seeking cooperation. Isaiah was bitterly indignant. "Woe to those who go down to Egypt for help and rely on horses", he cried, "but do not look to the Holy one of Israel or consult the Lord . . . The Egyptians are men, and not God; and their horses are flesh, and not spirit" (Isa. 31:1–3). But Hezekiah did not listen.

By 701, Sennacherib was free of his northern troubles and he could now take action against his rebellious southern vassals. (Hezekiah had no doubt foreseen this likelihood, and it was probably shortly before this that he fortified Jerusalem and built the Siloam tunnel, as mentioned earlier.) Sennacherib swept southwards with a formidable army and wrought havoc among the rebel states. When he reached Judah, he systematically began reducing its settlements. The Bible says that he "came up against all the fortified cities of Judah and took them" (II Kings 18:13 and Isa. 36:1), and Sennacherib's own records claim that he destroyed forty-six. When his army reached the gates of Jerusalem, he sent his representative ("the Rabshakeh", as he is called in the Bible) to demand Hezekiah's surrender.

There follows (in II Kings 18 and Isaiah 36) a fascinating story of how the Rabshakeh tried to weaken Hezekiah's resolve by an astute essay in psychological warfare. It is possible that this device was used instead of a straightforward, but lengthy, siege and assault because Sennacherib may have had to contend with the Egyptians and wanted Jerusalem, by then well fortified, neutralized first — and quickly. At all events, we are told that the Rabshakeh "came to Jerusalem . . . and stood by the conduit" and "called for the king" (II Kings 18:17, 18). Hezekiah sent three members of his household outside the walls to meet him. The Rabshakeh addressed them in a loud and commanding voice — and in the language of the Judeans — telling them to give this message from Sennacherib to Hezekiah: "On what do you rest this confidence of yours?. . . Behold, you are relying now on Egypt, that broken reed of a staff, which will pierce the hand of any man who leans on it . . . But if you say to me, 'We rely on the Lord our God' is it not He whose high places and altars Hezekiah has removed" — twisting Hezekiah's religious reform in removing the *pagan* altars. He went on to ask how Hezekiah could think of facing Sennacherib's army when he was clearly so weak that he had to depend "on Egypt for chariots and for horsemen". Finally, did he not understand that Sennacherib was carrying out the will of God? "Is it without the Lord that I have come up against this place to destroy it?" (II Kings 18:19–25).

Archaeologist Yigael Yadin points out that the Rabshakeh was "trying to shake the offensive spirit of the men of Jerusalem by seeking to undermine the three foundations upon which Hezekiah bases his resistance — the help of the Lord; the assistance of his ally Egypt; his own strength".

The derisive words of the Assyrian brought this immediate reaction from Hezekiah's officials: "Pray, speak to your servants in the Aramaic language, for we understand it; do not speak to us in the language of Judah within the hearing of the people who are on the wall" (II Kings 18:26). But this, says Yadin, was exactly the Rashbakeh's intention, speaking directly to the Judean defenders on the walls, and in the language they could understand, in order to undermine their confidence. It becomes clear in the Assyrian's response: "Has my master sent me to speak these words to your master and to you, and not to the men sitting on the wall, who are doomed with you to eat their own dung and dring their own urine?" (II Kings 18:27).

"This", writes Yigael Yadin, "is perhaps the earliest recorded example of psychological warfare, which follows the principle of appealing directly to the people and army, over the heads of their chiefs, rousing them to overthrow their leaders by the threat of severe

the commander... sent by Sargon the king of Assyria, came to Ashdod and fought against it and took it... Woe to those who go down to Egypt for help (Isaiah 20:1; 31:1)

A seated Philistine goddess in the form of a stone chair found at Ashdod. When the king of Ashdod was urged into conflict with Assyria by the promise of Egyptian help, Hezekiah was dissuaded by Isaiah from following suit. Ashdod, betrayed by Egypt, was destroyed.

action if they refuse and the promise of paradise if they acquiesce". For the Rabshakeh spoke even more loudly, telling the troops of Judah, in their own language: "Do not let Hezekiah deceive you, for he will not be able to deliver you out of my hand . . . Make your peace with me; then every one of you will eat of his own vine, and every one of his own fig tree, and every one of you will drink the water of his own cistern" (II Kings 18:28–31).

It was a dazzling effort — but it did not work. It is probable that Hezekiah himself had gone up to the wall and stood within earshot, though out of sight, of the envoy below. He would thus quickly have sensed the Assyrian's intentions, and given a appropriate order to his men, for the Bible says that they "were silent . . . for the king's command was, 'Do not answer him'". Nevertheless, when his three aides came, utterly shaken, "with their clothes rent" as if in mourning, to give him a detailed report of their meeting, Hezekiah was himself much disturbed, and he too "rent his clothes . . . and went into the house of the Lord" (Isa. 37:1). From there he sent to Isaiah for advice.

ISAIAH'S CRUCIAL ADVICE

This, however, did not mean that the king was wavering. He was almost certainly anxious to make a stand. He must anyway have known that he and the city could expect short shrift from Sennacherib even if he did give in without a struggle. The situation was indeed more desperate than it had ever been, and it is probable that he was also under pressure from court counsellors who were opposed to action. He had to take a decision, and it would be the most fateful decision of his life. In such circumstances he must have thought it well to hear the wisdom of the prophet. On past experience, he would have been justified in expecting Isaiah to recommend submission — for Isaiah had opposed all his earlier revolts and had been proved right. They had been rash and premature. He was probably surprised — and greatly heartened — when Isaiah's advice was to stand firm, to reject the surrender offer and to fight. "Do not be afraid because of the words that you have heard", Isaiah told him. "Concerning the king of Assyria, he shall not come into this city or shoot an arrow there, or come before it with a shield or cast up a siege mound against it. By the way that he came, by the same he shall return, and he shall not come into this city, says the Lord. For I will defend this city to save it . . ." (II Kings 19:6, 32–34).

Isaiah's words were crucial, giving Hezekiah just the confidence he needed. His answer to Sennacherib was resistance.

Elsewhere, the Assyrians were victorious. But Jerusalem was not taken. The siege was lifted, suddenly, mysteriously. The Bible notes two factors which would explain the unexpected departure of the enemy forces. One (in II Kings 19:35) was that they were smitten by a plague which decimated their ranks. The other (in II Kings 19:7) was that Sennacherib received information of a nature which made him hurry back to his capital, Nineveh.

[Certain difficulties in the biblical text — chapters 18 and 19 of II Kings and chapters 36 to 39 of Isaiah — leave it unclear as to whether Sennacherib conducted two major campaigns against Hezekiah's Judah or one. Most scholars now hold that there was only one, in 701, and that the two principal episodes recounted in the Bible are parallel accounts of the same action. A few, however, consider that the biblical text, together with what is known from contemporary records of the military and political situation in the area, make more feasible the supposition that Sennacherib struck twice, once in 701 and again in about the year 688, and that it was in the second campaign that Jerusalem was besieged and that Isaiah made his fateful intervention. We have followed the "one campaign" school. However, in terms of the influence of Isaiah, it does not matter which version is correct, for his words of advice are what counts, whether they were uttered in 701 or 688.]

Throughout the years of Assyrian danger, Isaiah called on king and people to turn from their godless and immoral ways, warning them of catastrophe unless they did. Assyria would be used as the instrument of divine retribution. "Assyria, the rod of my anger, the staff of my fury" (Isa. 10:5) would be sent against them; and Judah had indeed suffered greatly at the hands of this northern power. Why, then, did Isaiah alter his tone at the climactic moment?

The fact is that his teaching and his guidance, his words of enlightenment and of admonition, had taken root. Hezekiah was a more mature, wise and pious king than he had been when he ascended the throne, and Judah was a more just and devout society. Moreover, Assyria, with a voracious appetite for conquest, had begun to display an overweening insolence and pride, and Isaiah believed that the very instrument which had been used to afflict Judah would now be broken against the walls of its former victim. "This", says Isaiah, is now "the word that the Lord has spoken concerning [Sennacherib] .... Because you have raged against me and your arrogance has come into my ears, I will put my hook in your nose and my bit in your mouth, and I will turn you back on the way by which you came" (II Kings 19:28).

O Lord, ...hear all the words of Sennacherib, which he has sent to mock the living God *(Isaiah 37:17)*

Section of a relief on a wall panel in the palace of Sennacherib, the Assyrian monarch, at Nineveh, depicting his destruction of Lachish. He tried at the time to take Jerusalem by persuading Hezekiah to surrender, but the king, given confidence by the prophet Isaiah, refused, and the Assyrians withdrew.

In speaking out against Assyria as he did, Isaiah was concerned not only for the fate of Jerusalem but also for the welfare of all who suffered under imperialism. Indeed, as Professor Moshe Weinfeld has pointed out, Isaiah was the first man in history to protest against imperialism, by a brilliant combination of erudition and insight. Dr. Weinfeld shows (in a recently published study) that Isaiah often used and turned against them the very themes and expressions which the imperial tyrants had themselves used in their self-glorification, and which we know from the ancient annals of Assyria and Babylonia. Abundant historical and building records have come to us from the reign (705–681 BC) of Sennacherib, "the great king, king of the universe, king of Assyria". In one of the inscriptions, commemorating the completion of the armory near his great palace at Nineveh, Sennacherib boasts: "I sent the order to the kings of Amurru, all of them, who had submitted to me (*literally,* at my feet). Great cedar beams they felled in Mount Amanus, dragged them to Nineveh and roofed (my palaces with them). Door-leaves of cypress and liaru-wood

I covered with a sheathing of bronze and set them up in their doors . . ."

Isaiah would seem to be quoting directly from just such an inscription, with its references to "cedar beams" and "cypress" wood, when he cries: ". . . you have said, 'With my many chariots I have gone up the heights of the mountains, to the far recesses of Lebanon; I felled its tallest cedars, its choicest cypresses . . .'" (Isa. 37:24). Or again, looking to the day of imperial collapse, Isaiah says: "you will take up this taunt against" the tyrant . . . "How the oppressor has ceased . . . The Lord has broken the staff of the wicked, the sceptre of rulers, that smote the people in wrath with unceasing blows, that ruled the nations in anger with unrelenting persecution. The whole earth is at rest and quiet; they break forth into singing. The cypresses rejoice at you, the cedars of Lebanon, saying, 'Since you were laid low, no hewer comes up against us'" (Isa. 14:4–8).

Isaiah was also clearly familiar with the bombast of Sargon, father of Sennacherib. In what is known as the Display Inscription which stood on wall slabs of four salons in

In his classic tirade against imperialism, Isaiah foretold the downfall of Sennacherib and the collapse of his Assyrian empire. The Lord would "put my hook in your nose and my bit in your mouth". (Isaiah 37:29).

the palace Sargon had built at Dur-Sargina (now Khorsabad), there is an account of the events from the year of his accession to the fifteenth years of his reign. In it, "Sargon, the great king, the mighty king, king of the Universe, king of Assyria, viceroy of Babylon, king of Sumer and Akkad", boasts of his imperial power: "I smashed all enemy lands like pots, and cast bonds upon the four regions (of the earth). I opened up mighty mountains whose passes were difficult and countless, and I spied out their trails. By main force I advanced over inaccessible paths (in) steep and terrifying places, I crossed all (sorts of) plains". Then follows a list of all the countries he has overrun, and he concludes: "all of these I brought under my sway, over them I set my officers and governors, the yoke of my sovereignty I placed upon them".

Isaiah was reacting to precisely this kind of self-exaltation and to the phenomenon of imperialism when he says that the Lord "will punish the arrogant boasting of the king of Assyria and his haughty pride. For he says: 'By the strength of my hand I have done it . . . I have removed the boundaries of peoples, and have plundered their treasures; like a bull I have brought down those who sat on thrones. My hand has found like a nest the wealth of the peoples; and as men gather eggs that have been forsaken so I have gathered all the earth . . .'" But, says Isaiah, "under his glory a burning will be kindled, like the burning of a fire" (Isa. 10:12, 16).

Isaiah was a contemporary of Sargon and Sennacherib, and he would have heard the tales of Middle Eastern travellers who had seen the edifices built by these monarchs, and who would have relayed the words they had seen in the display inscriptions. It is through the perception of Dr. Weinfeld that we now see a direct link between the texts of the emperors and Isaiah's tirades against imperialism. Weinfeld has also shown that Isaiah is often quoting directly from the imperialists' boasts, beginning his utterance with "For he says" (Isa. 10:13) — "he" being the monarch; or, addressing the tyrant directly, "You said in your heart . . . I will set my throne on high" (14:13); or, speaking of Sennacherib, "you have said" (37:24), prefatory to the emperor's vainglorious declarations.

These protests against imperialism, delivered by Isaiah with such vigor and eloquence, go well with the prophet's idea — and he was the first to express this, too — of a world not dominated by physical imperialist might but ruled by the spirit, a world of universal peace, "of wisdom and understanding", where the nations will accept decisions by their own will, persuaded not by sword or whip but by "mouth" and "the breath of . . . lips" (Isa. 11:2-4).

Jerusalem was untaken. Its deliverance was acclaimed as a divine miracle. Its survival against so mighty a foe, the one fortress-city to remain standing when all others in the path of the conqueror had fallen, gave it a special mystique. Here alone the Assyrians had been held. The Temple was intact. At the instant of decision, the words of Isaiah, the man of God, had tipped the scales and saved the city. The feeling spread that Jerusalem was inviolable. In physical terms, this article of faith was to receive a tragic jolt just over a hundred years later. In spiritual

Nineveh... in which there are more than a hundred and twenty thousand persons who do not know their right hand from their left (Jonah 4:11)

The Royal palaces at Nineveh, the ancient capital of the Assyrian empire on the eastern bank of the river Tigris opposite the modern city of Mosul. The restoration is by James Ferguson.

terms — Jerusalem in the heart of every Jew — it remains alive to this day. It was the prodigious influence of Isaiah which helped to sustain the supremacy of Jerusalem as the centre of the Hebrew nation.

Biblical scholars had long been perplexed by the difference in tone and content between the early and later chapters of the Book of Isaiah. The first part fits events which occurred in the latter part of the 8th and beginning of the 7th centuries BC, and the style is more trenchant. The second part clearly relates to the period following the destruction of Jerusalem, and the style is more gentle. Modern scholars now suggest that of its 66 chapters, the first 36 are unmistakably the authentic voice of the 8th century prophet. Chapters 36 to 39 correspond to chapters 18 to 20 of II Kings and are considered to be Isaiah's words as recorded by his disciples — he is referred to in the third person. Chapters 40 to 66 (with a new note struck in the opening lines of chapter 40: "Comfort, comfort my people, says your God. Speak tenderly to Jerusalem . . .") are said to be the work of a 6th century prophet, close to

The cypresses rejoice at you... saying, 'Since you were laid low, no hewer comes up against us' (Isaiah 14:8)

Sargon II (left), king of Assyria, father of Sennacherib, and conqueror of Samaria in 722 BC. This head was found at excavations of his palace in Dur-Sargina (Sargon's city), today's Khorsabad. Sennacherib boasted that he ordered the kings he had conquered to cut down cypress trees (right) and drag them to Nineveh to provide doors for his palaces.

Isaiah in spirit and power of thought and expression, who was addressing his fellow Jews not in their own state but in Babylonian exile, consoling them in their calamity, urging them to preserve their identity and their faith, and offering the hope of their return. He may even have been witness to their restoration in Jerusalem and Judah in the days of Cyrus. Traditionalists, however, hold to the view that the entire Book is the work of the one and only Isaiah of the 8th century, and that the later chapters are the projection of the prophet's vision into the future.

6. PRESERVERS OF THE FAITH

Doom, doom. That was the word most frequently on the lips of the prophets in the late 7th century BC. None expressed this warning with greater consistency or more pungent urgency than Jeremiah, the man who most nearly approaches Isaiah in calibre and influence. He is indeed considered by many to be Isaiah's peer, and the similarity in their qualities is striking — poetic genius, foresight, passion, courage, integrity. Both had a decisive impact on the future of their people. Both inveighed against paganism and injustice and warned of disaster if there were no return to righteousness. Both were heavily involved in the turbulent political and military events of their times and were outspoken to their monarchs. Both were the dominant spirits of their day in Jerusalem, and the public activities of each spanned half a century. But Jeremiah's pattern of life was different from that of the earlier prophet, and so, in certain spheres, was the nature of his utterances. Isaiah suffered inwardly over the iniquities he witnessed, but he was subjected to no maltreatment, and he was respected even by his opponents. Jeremiah, in addition to suffering an almost chronic anguish of soul, was reviled, mocked, harried, imprisoned. As for their teaching, Isaiah warned of punishment but felt that Jerusalem and the nation would escape the ultimate calamity, and he envisioned a wondrous society once the people returned to God. Jeremiah lived with unceasing forebodings of physical doom — Jerusalem would not be saved and the nation would be thrust into exile, though he also thought that if they kept alive the spirit of their faith, they would return. At the moment of supreme crisis, Isaiah urged resistance, and he was heeded. At a similar moment, though admittedly when the pressures were heavier, Jeremiah considered resistance fruitless and advised delay, but he was ignored. Isaiah could end an eventful life content in the knowledge that the nation and its centre had been spared. Jeremiah witnessed the destruction of Jerusalem and his life was a sorrow from beginning to end.

POLITICAL UPHEAVAL

The differences between these two prophetic giants are a reflection of the changes in circumstances of the Judah of Jeremiah from the Judah of Isaiah. The intervening years saw violent upheavals in the region, wrought by the clash of empires, and these forged the far more sombre epoch in which Jeremiah and his prophetic contemporaries gave voice to their dark pronouncements.

Isaiah died about the same time as king Hezekiah (687 BC) in a triumph of resistance against the Assyrians. But the Assyrians were bound to react as soon as they felt free — their power was now reaching its peak — and it was this no doubt which prompted Hezekiah's son Manasseh (687–642) to repudiate his father's resistance policy. Throughout his reign, Judah remained a passive vassal, and this obviously influenced the religious life of Judah, with the recognition of Assyrian gods, the introduction of pagan worship and customs even within the Temple, and the abandonment of Hezekiah's reforms. His son Amon (642–640) followed this docile policy. He was assassinated, possibly by anti-Assyrian elements in the kingdom, after a reign of only two years, and his young son Josiah (640–609) was crowned king. It was under Josiah

that Judah's fortunes rose; for only a few years after he reached the throne, Assyria began to decline. Her mighty empire was by now over-extended, and since she was again beset by troubles from a resurgent Babylon and a revived Egypt, she was unable to maintain strict control over her dependent territories which lay between them.

Judah was once again free; and, taking further advantage of Assyrian weakness, Josiah marched north and took possession of the Assyrian provinces which had formerly constituted the kingdom of Israel. His most notable step, however, was to cast out the Assyrian and other pagan deities — in itself symbolic of the renunciation of the imperial yoke — as part of a religious reform more thoroughgoing than that of Hezekiah. This reform was spurred by the powerful words of Zephaniah and Jeremiah. It received a notable boost by the discovery of a sacred "book of the law" (II Kings 22:8) or "book of the covenant" (II Kings 23:2) in the Temple while it was being purified, repaired and renovated. Scholars agree that this was some form of the biblical Book of Deuteronomy,

The words of Jeremiah… of Anathoth… They will fight against you; but they shall not prevail against you, for I am with you, says the Lord, to deliver you (Jeremiah 1:1, 19)

The village of Anathoth (left) just north of Jerusalem where the prophet Jeremiah was born. Rembrandt's Jeremiah (below). The prophet foresees the destruction of Jerusalem in this great biblical painting by the 17th century Dutch master.

Woe to him who builds his house by unrighteousness (Jeremiah 22:13)

Decorative capital from a palace-citadel (below)
discovered at the archaeological excavations
at Ramat Rachel (left) on the outskirts
of Jerusalem. It is believed to have been built
with forced labour by king Jehoiakim,
which provoked a furious outburst
from Jeremiah.

General view of the valley of Jezreel taken from the ruins of ancient Megiddo where the righteous king Josiah was killed in combat. Megiddo commands a strategic pass and was the site of countless battles. Armageddon, envisioned as the site of the last great battle to be fought at the end of time, is a corruption of Har Megiddo, Hebrew for the Hill of Megiddo.

and the king was overwhelmed by its stern warnings against the neglect of its laws. He was moved to take urgent measures to fulfil its commands, banning all pagan altars in Judah and the territory of former Israel, shutting down rural shrines and centralizing the national worship in Jerusalem. At the next pilgrim festival of Passover, all the people of Judah and Israel came to Jerusalem to celebrate. It was prepared "according to the word of the Lord by Moses" and "No passover like it had been kept in Israel since the days of Samuel the prophet; none of the kings of Israel had kept such a passover as was kept by Josiah, and the priests and the Levites, and all Judah and Israel who were present, and the inhabitants of Jerusalem" (II Chron. 25:6, 18).

There were undoubtedly political aspects to Josiah's religious reforms. They were a tangible demonstration of independence from Assyria. Centralized worship in the Jerusalem Temple underlined the re-union of the Hebrew peoples, Israel and Judah, as in David's time. And Josiah assuredly found political encouragement in stressing the apparent con-

*go out to the valley of the son of Hinnom... and proclaim...
'Hear the word of the Lord, O kings of Judah and inhabitants
of Jerusalem'* (Jeremiah 19:2-3)

firmation of the Lord's promise to David that he had chosen Jerusalem, Zion, as his dwelling place and that David's dynasty would be uninterrupted, with each successor king enjoying divine protection. (The kings of Judah were consistently of the Davidic line.) However, the basic impulse of the reforms was religious, and for this, as we have observed, the ground had been prepared by Zephaniah and Jeremiah (though they would have had reservations about some of the political implications).

The prophet Zephaniah, a few years older than Jeremiah, stands more in the tradition of Isaiah. He denounced the idolatry and injustice which had flourished under Manasseh and Amon; railed against the "judges" who were "evening wolves that leave nothing till the morning"; against the official "prophets" who "are wanton, faithless men" and the "priests" who "profane what is sacred" and "do violence to the law" (Zeph. 3:3, 4); and against "the officials and the king's sons and all who array themselves in foreign attire"; but with repentance, and after passing through a refinement of divine judgement,

he believed, with Isaiah, that a righteous remnant would remain: "those who are left in Israel; they shall do no wrong and utter no lies" and "shall seek refuge in the name of the Lord" (Zeph. 3:12, 13).

THE ANGUISH OF JEREMIAH

The Book of Zephaniah gives no details of the prophet's background. Of Jeremiah, however, we know that he was born in the village of Anathoth, some three miles northeast of Jerusalem, in the latter part of the reign of Manasseh. He came of a priestly family, which could probably trace its descent back to Abiathar, the priest in David's time whose home was also Anathoth, and through him back to the high priest Eli of Shiloh. This would explain his having been reared in the earliest Israelite tradition and all his preaching is informed by the paramount need of the nation to conform to the Mosaic Covenant. He thus welcomed the discovery of the sacred "book of the law" and Josiah's efforts to reinstate its obligations gave him no doubt the only joy he was ever to experience. Josiah indeed comes in for special praise as a man

Babylon was a golden cup in the Lord's hand, making all the earth drunken; the nations drank of her wine, therefore the nations went mad (Jeremiah 51:7)

A reconstruction of the ancient city of
Babylon at the time of Nebuchadnezzar, who
destroyed Jerusalem and the Temple.
A royal procession is passing the Ishtar Gate
on its way to the palace. The hanging
gardens of Babylon may be seen on the roof
of the palace (upper right), and the Tower
of Babel in the distance.

who did "justice and righteouness ... He judged the cause of the poor and needy; then it was well" (Jer. 22:15, 16). At the time, too, he applauded the king's measures to achieve the religious and political re-unification of Israel and Judah, welcoming the "day when watchmen will call in the hill country of Ephraim: 'Arise, and let us go up to Zion, to the Lord our God'" (Jer. 31:6). Later, he was to lose hope that Zion would physically survive the next imperial onslaught, despite the divine promise to David, for that promise was contingent on the people's fulfilment of their earlier obligation under the Mosaic Covenant.

This happened during the reign of Jehoiakim, a son of Josiah, when the political pattern in the region had undergone a violent change, and an anguished Jeremiah, his heart burdened by disillusionment, gave inspired utterance to his premonition of doom. Judah's wheel of fortune had turned full circle. Josiah had died in 609, killed at Megiddo in battle against the Egyptians. In the previous three years, Assyria had been dealt a series of crippling blows by Babylon, losing its capital,

Nineveh, and then Haran, to which its government had fled. The other vulture hovering over the dying Assyrian empire was Egypt, and, alarmed at the victories of her rival contender, she decided to support the gasping Assyrians and eject the Babylonians from Haran. A large force under Pharaoh Neco II accordingly proceeded north to join her new Assyrian allies at Carchemish, on the Euphrates. At this point Josiah acted. An Egyptian-Assyrian victory would give the rising Egypt a free hand in the region, and he, who had thrown off the Assyrian yoke, would find himself subservient to Egypt. He therefore resolved to stop the Egyptian army — which would also put him in the good graces of Babylon — and Megiddo was where the military meeting took place. Judah was defeated by the Egyptians and the dead Josiah was brought back to Jerusalem in his chariot. (Archaeological excavations at Megiddo show that it was destroyed at that time.) The Pharaoh continued northward to the Euphrates, and though his attack on the Babylonians failed, he established control of the intermediate lands. Judah was one of them, and

171

Then... Hananiah took the yoke-bars from the neck of Jeremiah the prophet, and broke them *(Jeremiah 28:10)*

Like a yoked ox at plough, Jeremiah harnessed himself with thongs and yoke-bars to dramatize his recommended policy of temporary submission to Babylon, foreseeing disaster in revolt.

three months after Josiah's death, his son and successor, Jehoahaz, was summoned to the Pharaoh's northern headquarters and deported to Egypt. His brother Jehoiakim (609–598) was enthroned in his stead as an Egyptian vassal.

The shock to the people of Judah was devastating. With the independence gained by Josiah lost, a reaction set in against his religious reforms — for they had not saved the kingdom — and the weak Jehoiakim allowed them to lapse. It is evident from Jeremiah that there was a return to pagan practices and moral laxity. At the same time, those who had opposed the reforms in Josiah's time now claimed that the return to the earlier Mosaic Covenant had been a mistake, and offered the reassurance that this had been superseded by the Lord's promise to David. Jerusalem and the Temple would be protected. It was this popular illusion which Jeremiah sought to destroy, arguing in words of fierce majesty that persistence in their distorted theology and a return to moral and religious corruption would save neither the Temple nor Jerusalem — nor them.

Jehoiakim was a disaster, and Jeremiah's outspoken attacks provoked royal reprisals. But this did not stop the prophet. He was particularly scathing when the king, apparently haring more for his comfort than the welfare of his subjects, decided to build himself a new palace-citadel, using forced labour. "Woe to him", cried Jeremiah, "who builds his house by unrighteousness, and his upper room by injustice; who makes his neighbour serve him for nothing, and does not give him his wages; who says, 'I will build myself a great house...'" (Jer. 22:13, 14).

Jeremiah would often stand in the court of the Temple and, addressing the worshippers, publicly assail the religious and the royal establishments. On one occasion, the chief priest "beat Jeremiah the prophet, and put him in the stocks that were in the upper Benjamin Gate of the house of the Lord". But he was released next day, unrepentant. On another occasion, after warning the public that an iniquitous Jerusalem would be destroyed, just as God had destroyed the shrine-city of Shiloh some 450 years earlier, he narrowly escaped the death sentence. (A

pious priest who echoed a similar warning was not so fortunate.) Sometimes he would perform a symbolic act — a common feature of the ancient east — to dramatize his words, such as taking an earthenware jar before an assembly in Jerusalem's valley of Hinnom, dashing it to the ground, and crying out: "Thus says the Lord of hosts: so will I break this people and this city, as one breaks a potter's vessel".

THE EVE OF DISASTER

In the year 605 the Babylonians under Nebuchadnezzar inflicted a crushing defeat on the Egyptians at Carchemish and soon gained control of the lands of the former Assyrian empire, including those which had recently come under tribute to Egypt. Within two years, Judah had become a vassal of Babylon, subservient once again to a northern, Mesopotamian empire. In 601, however, after an indecisive battle against the Egyptians near their frontier, Nebuchadnezzar returned north to reorganize his forces, and some of his vassals, prodded by Egypt, seized the occasion to revolt. Judah was one of them.

Jeremiah and others had urged the king against such a step. The prophet, it is true, expressed his views in religious terms, but they were clearly based on an astute political appraisal of the political and military situation. In his estimate of the rival imperial strengths, Jeremiah had come to the conclusion that Babylon was very much on the rise, that the battle on the Egyptian frontier had proved nothing, and that Nebuchadnezzar would soon return, vanquish Egypt and take revenge on all who had rebelled. It was dangerous, therefore, to heed the blandishments of Egypt. Of course he wanted independence as much as Jehoiakim. But the time was not yet ripe. Babylon would eventually overreach herself, and then would be the time to strike. But not yet. In his prophetic style, the way Jeremiah put it was that Babylon — like Assyria in Isaiah's time — had been used as an instrument of divine punishment against the iniquities of Judah. Eventually, however, she would in turn be broken: Nebuchadnezzar who "has devoured . . . crushed . . . swallowed . . . filled his belly" (Jer. 51:34) would be forced to disgorge his acquisitions and "wild beasts shall dwell with hyenas in Babylon" (Jer. 50:39).

Jehoiakim appraised the situation differently, and rejected Jeremiah's advice. With small countries squeezed between two rival powers, then as now, an unwise decision on a major issue at a critical moment could mean the difference between survival and destruction. The king's decision proved rash. In 598, Nebuchadnezzar again marched south and by the time he reached Jerusalem, Jehoiakim was dead (possibly assassinated by those who hoped to assuage Babylonian anger and thereby secure more lenient treatment). No Egyptian help had been forthcoming. Jehoiakim was succeeded by his teenage son Jehoiachin who surrendered the city and was carried off to Babylon, together with the queen mother, the royal household, leading citizens (including the prophet Ezekiel), army commanders, technicians and craftsmen, numbering several thousands, as well as much booty. In place of Jehoiachin, the Babylonians placed his uncle on the throne. This was Zedekiah (597–587), a brother of Jehoiakim.

This tragic young man was well-intentioned but weak, and he had now been elevated to head his nation in its grimmest hour when what was required was a forthright leader of experience and sagacity. Zedekiah found himself torn between the conflicting moods and opinions of officials and public. The spirit of revolt still simmered, and there was a majority feeling that Jehoiachin, looked up to as the legitimate king although in exile, would return together with the other captives. This was encouraged by the official priesthood who believed that the descendant of David would be divinely rescued. Furthermore, Judah had lost territory, with some of its cities laid waste and others, like Lachish, severely damaged. The hope was strong that they would be resuscitated and the will was strong to make the kingdom whole again. Jeremiah led the minority view that the time for revolt was not yet propitious. Babylon was still too powerful, and Judean society was still far from spotless. There was anguished urgency in his denunciations of the over-confident militants whose precipitate rebellion could bring only ruin.

עמוד ימין

ארמנותיה

כי כה אמר יהוה צבאות
כרתו עצה ושפכו על
ירושלם סללה זאת העיר
הפקד כלה בקרבה
כהקיר בור מימיה כן הקרה
רעתה חמס ושד ישמע
בה על פני תמיד חלי ומכה
הוסרי ירושלם פן תקע
נפשי ממך פן אשימך
שממה ארץ לוא נושבה
כה אמר יהוה צבאות
עולל יעוללו כגפן שארית
ישראל השב ידך כבוצר
על סלסלות אל מי אדברה
ואעידה וישמעו הנה ערלה
אזנם ולא יוכלו להקשיב
הנה דבר יהוה היה להם
לחרפה לא יחפצו בו ואת
חמת יהוה מלאתי נלאתי
הכיל שפך על עולל בחוץ
ועל סוד בחורים יחדו כי
גם איש עם אשה ילכדו
זקן עם מלא ימים ונסבו
בתיהם לאחרים שדות
ונשים יחדו כי אטה את
ידי על ישבי הארץ נאם
יהוה כי מקטנם ועד גדולם
כלם בוצע בצע מנביא ועד
כהן כלו עשה שקר

עמוד שמאל — טור ימין

וירפאו את שבר עמי על
נקלה לאמר שלום שלום
ואין שלום הבישו כי תועבה
עשו גם בוש לא יבושו גם
הכלים לא ידעו לכן יפלו
בנפלים בעת פקדתים
יכשלו אמר יהוה
כה אמר יהוה עמדו
על דרכים וראו ושאלו
לנתבות עולם אי זה דרך
הטוב ולכו בה ומצאו מרגוע
לנפשכם ואמרו לא נלך
והקמתי עליכם צפים
הקשיבו לקול שופר ויאמרו
לא נקשיב לכן שמעו
הגוים ודעי עדה את אשר
בם שמעי הארץ הנה
אנכי מביא רעה אל העם הזה
פרי מחשבותם כי על
דברי לא הקשיבו ותורתי
וימאסו בה למה זה לי
לבונה משבא תבוא וקנה
הטוב מארץ מרחק
עלתיכם לא לרצון וזבחיכם
לא ערבו לי
לכן כה אמר יהוה הנני
נתן אל העם הזה מכשלים
וכשלו בם אבות ובנים יחדו
שכן ורעו אבדו כה אמר
יהוה הנה עם בא מארץ

עמוד שמאל — טור אמצעי

צפון וגוי גדול יעור מירכתי
ארץ קשת וכידון יחזיקו
אכזרי הוא ולא ירחמו
קולם כים יהמה ועל סוסים
ירכבו ערוך כאיש למלחמה
עליך בת ציון שמענו את
שמעו רפו ידינו צרה
החזיקתנו חיל כיולדה
אל תצאי השדה ובדרך
אל תלכי כי חרב לאיב
מגור מסביב בת עמי חגרי
שק והתפלשי באפר
אבל יחיד עשי לך מספד
תמרורים כי פתאם יבא
השדד עלינו בחון נתתיך
בעמי מבצר ותדע ובחנת
את דרכם כלם סרי
סוררים הלכי רכיל נחשת
וברזל כלם משחיתים
המה נחר מפח מאשתם
עפרת לשוא צרף צרוף
ורעים לא נתקו כסף
נמאס קראו להם כי מאס
יהוה בהם
הדבר אשר היה אל
ירמיהו מאת יהוה לאמר
עמד בשער בית יהוה
וקראת שם את הדבר
הזה ואמרת שמעו דבר
יהוה כל יהודה הבאים

עמוד שמאל — טור שמאל

כשערים האלה להשתחות
ליהוה כה אמר יהוה
צבאות אלהי ישראל היטיבו
דרכיכם ומעלליכם
ואשכנה אתכם במקום
הזה אל תבטחו לכם אל
דברי השקר לאמר היכל
יהוה היכל יהוה היכל יהוה
המה כי אם היטיב תיטיבו
את דרכיכם ואת מעלליכם
אם עשו תעשו משפט
בין איש ובין רעהו גר יתום
ואלמנה לא תעשקו ודם
נקי אל תשפכו במקום
הזה ואחרי אלהים אחרים
לא תלכו לרע לכם ושכנתי
אתכם במקום הזה בארץ
אשר נתתי לאבותיכם למן
עולם ועד עולם הנה אתם
בטחים לכם על דברי
השקר לבלתי הועיל הגנב
רצח ונאף והשבע לשקר
וקטר לבעל והלך אחרי
אלהים אחרים אשר לא
ידעתם ובאתם ועמדתם
לפני בבית הזה אשר נקרא
שמי עליו ואמרתם נצלנו
למען עשות את כל התועבת
האלה המערת פרצים
היה הבית הזה אשר נקרא

Passages from the Book of Jeremiah in the 13th century Bible copied in beautiful Hebrew script by a noted Jewish scribe in Spain in the 13th century. This Bible is known as the Damascus Keter (keter is Hebrew for crown) as for many centuries it was the pride of the Damascus Synagogue. It is now in Jerusalem.

He was shouted down, the more vehemently when news arrived of a rebellion inside Babylon itself. The revolt was quickly mastered, but it had inspired other vassals also to think of anti-Babylonian action, and Edom, Moab, Ammon, Tyre and Sidon sent ambassadors to Jerusalem to concert arrangements for a combined uprising. Jeremiah's reaction was to walk about with "thongs and yoke-bars" (Jer. 27:2) on his neck, to symbolize his recommended policy of submission for the time being. He also addressed himself both to his own people and to the vassal envoys, urging them not to "listen to your prophets, your diviners, your dreamers, your soothsayers, or your sorcerers, who are saying to you, 'You shall not serve the king of Babylon'. For it is a lie which they are prophesying to you" (Jer. 27:9, 10). Premature action would result in all being overrun and their peoples exiled. If they held still, they would remain on their "own land, to till it and dwell there" (Jer. 27:11).

Whether or not he was listened to on this occasion one cannot know; but there was no allied revolt. Nevertheless, one of the outstanding members of the religious establishment, Hananiah, violently opposed to Jeremiah's political views, took a leaf out of the prophet's notebook and, at a gathering in the Temple court, "took the yoke-bars from off the neck of Jeremiah the prophet, and broke them . . . saying, 'Thus says the Lord: Even so will I break the yoke of Nebuchadnezzar king of Babylon'" (Jer. 28:10, 11). Jeremiah said "Amen! May the Lord do so; may the Lord make the words which you have prophesied come true" (Jer. 28:6). But he thought, alas, that this was a false prophecy, comforting but illusory. And "Jeremiah the prophet went his way", says the Bible, simply, and one can picture this gaunt figure leaving the assembly after responding to Hananiah, bowed and sad, his heart bursting with love for his people and the wish to reassure them, but unable, through the depth of his honesty, to do so. The Hananiahs could encourage the people with hopeful words. But they were dangerous, for they instilled in the populace a false sense of optimism, and Jeremiah's reading of the situation showed that there were no grounds for optimism. Integrity forbade him to be glib; and his sense of duty prohibited him from remaining silent. It was Jeremiah's agonizing task to tell the public the grim truth: they were not yet ready, and they would have to bear subservience for the time being. This has ever been the mark of the great leader, the man of wisdom and of conscience who does not court popularity but who determines his course in accordance with the realities and follows it, no matter how unpleasant and unpopular.

Jeremiah almost broke under the burden. He could see the effect of his words. A few people were impressed. The king vacillated. Most of his officials were appalled. The Temple priests were shocked. And the public, desperate for freedom, were openly derisive. The prophet was only human, and all this told on him. He suffered fits of depression in which he cried out to the Lord that his words had become "a reproach and derision", and "I have become a laughingstock . . . every one mocks me" (Jer. 20:7, 8). Sometimes it was all too much and he cursed "the day on which I was born . . . Why did I come forth from the womb to see toil and sorrow, and spend my days in shame?" (Jer. 20:14, 18). But he could not repress his thoughts nor muzzle his lips. He had to speak out.

589 was a year in which he spoke out most fiercely. That was the year in which Zedekiah, taking the step which Jeremiah had so feared and warned against, hurled Judah into open revolt against mighty Babylon. Nebuchadnezzar reacted promptly and sent his forces south on a punitive expedition. When news of their march reached Jerusalem, Zedekiah, apparently having second thoughts, sent for guidance to the prophet whose earlier advice he had ignored. Jeremiah sent back word to the king that a rising was still premature. The people were neither spiritually nor militarily prepared. The struggle would be hopeless and, if persisted in, would end in devastation. However, the popular and official mood was one of resistance, and the king complied. The Babylonians reached Jerusalem early in 588, and put the city under siege. Life in the capital was grim, and Jeremiah courted even greater unpopularity, and no little danger, by continuing to express his familiar views. He was a demoralizing element, and there were moves to suppress him.

THE LETTERS OF LACHISH

Meanwhile, maintaining a holding unit round Jerusalem, the Babylonian army went through Judah on a relentless campaign of destruction, reducing every major city. Lachish was again one of them, and there was an echo of its destruction — and of Jeremiah's pessimistic words in the preceding months — in some startling archaeological discoveries. Excavations carried out at the site of this ancient Judean city in 1932–1938 yielded the celebrated "Lachish Letters", eighteen ostraca — inscribed potsherds — found in the early 6th century BC level among the burnt debris in a guard-room of a bastion in the outer city wall. Just over one hundred years after the Assyrian emperor Sennacherib (in 701) had attacked the town and recorded the battle scenes in the noted reliefs on the walls of his palace in Nineveh, the resettled Lachish had been partially destroyed by Nebuchadnezzar (in 598–597) and now, in his second invasion, completely destroyed. The letters were found in the period level *the army of the king of Babylon was fighting against Jerusalem and against all the cities of Judah that were left, Lachish and Azekah* (Jeremiah 34:7)

The archaeological mound of ancient Lachish (below), one of the cities of Judah destroyed by Nebuchadnezzar, king of Babylon. More than a hundred years earlier it had been rebuilt and resettled by the Jews after they had suffered siege and conquest by the Assyrian emperor Sennacherib, who recorded his victory in a relief (right) in his palace at Nineveh.

One of the "Lachish Letters", found among the 80 inscribed potsherds at archaeological excavations of the site in the 1930s. It was written by a subordinate officer to the Jewish commander of Lachish shortly before the final attack and destruction of the city by Nebuchadnezzar in 587 BC.

between those two actions. They were written in black ink on broken pottery and the language was classical Hebrew. They consisted for the most part of reports written in the years 588–587 to Yaosh, military commander of the fortress-city, by his subordinate officer, Hoshaiah, who was in command of an outpost to the north of Lachish. All these reports reflect the pessimism of the king — echoing Jeremiah — in Jerusalem at the time. One in particular refers to "the letter of the king and the letters of the princes" which the commander had received from Jerusalem and sent on to his subordinate with the note: "Pray read them". Hoshaiah does so and sends back this bitter comment: "And behold the words of the princes are not good, but to weaken our hands and to slacken the hands of the men who are informed about them . . . truly since thy servant read the letters there hath been no peace for thy servant . . ."

Suddenly, hope leapt high in Jerusalem. The Babylonians had heard a rumour that an Egyptian force was on its way, and they went to meet it. The siege was unexpectedly lifted. All were overjoyed, their resistance policy so gloriously vindicated. Their city was clearly under divine protection. Jeremiah alone remained unmoved. "Do not deceive yourselves" (Jer. 37:9), he told them. Like Isaiah before him, he had no faith in the Egyptians. They would retreat behind their own borders and the Babylonians would return. The reasoning behind his argument was ignored but his pacifist conclusion was seized upon and he was reviled. When he tried to leave the city to attend to some family property in his native village, he was arrested for attempting to desert to the enemy. Despite his angry denial "they beat him and imprisoned him in the . . . dungeon cells" (Jer. 37:15, 16).

After he had been there "many days", king Zedekiah had him brought secretly from the prison to the palace and anxiously enquired whether there was "any word from the Lord". Jeremiah said there was, and told him fearlessly, braving the supreme penalty for what could have been construed as treason: "You shall be delivered into the hand of the king of Babylon" (Jer. 37:17). It seems probable that, despite the sudden relief from Babylonian pressure, the king had also concluded that it was only temporary. He had no doubt begun to reflect that perhaps Jeremiah had been right after all. That was why he had sent for the prophet now, and why he received Jeremiah's words not with anger but with deepened dismay. He must have wished to surrender, but foresaw difficulties with his militants. At all events, he responded gently when Jeremiah having replied to the king's immediate enquiry, protested at his imprisonment, and then pleaded that at least he not be returned to the dungeon. The king agreed and committed him instead to "the court of the guard: and a loaf of bread was given him daily . . ." (Jer. 37:21).

The prophet apparently continued his preaching to the guards, and the nobles and the official priests brought pressure on the king to give them a free hand with this man who was endangering the morale of the troops. Zedekiah reluctantly agreed, and they cast him into a deep muddy cistern and left him there to die. But a sympathetic palace official reported to the king what they had done, and

the king told him to take three servants and "lift Jeremiah the prophet out of the cistern before he dies" (Jer. 38:10). They did so, and returned him to the court of the guard.

Zedekiah then arranged a further meeting with the prophet, again held in secret, and again asked for his latest appraisal of the situation and for his advice. Jeremiah could only repeat his previous words: surrender, and he and the city would be saved; continue resistance, and all would be destroyed. But willing as he was, Zedekiah felt unable to follow the prophet's advice. He was too weak to impose his will on a population brimming with the spirit of resistance and in no mood for defeatist talk. Jeremiah was returned to his guards, and there he remained.

Nebuchadnezzar's forces soon returned. Either the Egyptian move had been no more than a rumour, or their army had been quickly defeated. Attempts to breach the walls were heroically repulsed. The embattled Jerusalemites fought stubbornly month after month. Their food rations steadily dwindled but there was no talk of surrender. They would fight to the last. And they did, right up to the midsummer of 587 when the Babylonians effected a breach just as the food supplies ran out. The city fell. Zedekiah escaped but was caught in the plains of Jericho. Taken to Nebuchadnezzar's headquarters in the north, he was made to witness the execution of his sons and then his eyes were put out, and he was carried off to a Babylonian prison where he died. In Jerusalem, the leading nobles, army commanders, civilian officials, chief Temple priests and prominent citizens were killed. The Temple treasures were taken to Babylon. The city was then systematically destroyed: the Temple, palace, all large buildings and Jerusalem's walls were razed. The bulk of the survivors were exiled to Babylon. Almost the only ones left were "some of the poorest of the land to be vine-dressers and ploughmen" (II Kings 25:12).

Also left was Jeremiah. Nebuchadnezzar had given orders that he be spared — under the mistaken notion that the prophet was pro-Babylonian because he had opposed resistance. His friend Gedaliah was appointted governor of devastated Judah, now incorpo-rated into the Babylonian empire, and he established his office in Mizpah, a few miles north of the ruined capital. A heartbroken Jeremiah joined him there. A few months later, Gedaliah was assassinated. His loyal friends, unable to catch the murderer, and fearing they would be blamed by Babylon, decided to seek refuge in Egypt. Jeremiah pleaded with them not to, but they insisted; and anxious for his fate if he were left behind, they took him with them. There he died.

VOICES OF HOPE
This was the dramatic political and military background against which were set the visionary words of Jeremiah and the other prophets of his period, Zephaniah, Nahum, Habakkuk and — the greatest of his contemporaries, Ezekiel. None was a political figure in the narrow sense of being wholly concerned with changing government policy. Jeremiah of course tried this, as we have seen; but if that were all, he would today be no more than a name on a list of colorful figures with a walk-on part on some distant stage of history. To him and his prophetic colleagues,

Interior of the cave of Zedekiah, where
the king is believed to have hidden during
his attempted escape from Jerusalem
when it fell to the Babylonians.

however, political action was but one facet of their larger preoccupation with the destiny of the nation and with moulding the minds of their people to meet their challenge at all times in the future; and in this they succeeded.

These inspired men, viewing developments in the region with greater clarity and foresight than the professional politicians, saw the small Jewish State being crushed between the forces of the two rival empires. The danger might be avoided by a nimble and sagacious foreign policy, coupled with a firm domestic policy which could root out corruption, indifference and a hankering for pagan temptations, restore the religious ideals of justice and piety, and gird the people to face their moral obligations. But neither the king nor the official priesthood seemed competent or willing to pursue these unpopular policies. The result, as the prophets saw, could only be the loss of the state, death and exile. It meant doom, of course, for that generation. But did it mean the doom of the nation? The answer of the prophets was a passionate No, and they sought in all their utterances not only to guide the people on their current

behavior but also to show whoever might survive the imminent tragedy how to cope with its fearful implications. In so doing, they pointed the way to the preservation of the Jewish faith and of the Jewish identity under all conditions, even in exile, and to the eventual restoration of Jewish independence in their land.

The basic implication of the tragic events for the survivors in Babylonian exile was that they had been abandoned by God. This had been their compelling thought as they trudged under guard on their long hot prison-trek to their new, unfamiliar, northern destination. They were stunned to the depths of their souls. Physical hardship they could endure, and accept. Their society had failed in its religious and moral obligations, and punishment was in order. But destruction? They had behaved no worse than many of the previous generations since the Israelite settlement more than 600 years earlier, yet these had never been swept from the land. At the critical moment, the Lord had always remembered His promise. True, the kingdom of Israel had been wiped out 140 years before, but they

186

the army of the Chaldeans pursued them and overtook Zedekiah in the plains of Jericho *(Jeremiah 39:5)*

The Judean wilderness between Jerusalem and Jericho where Zedekiah emerged from hiding and fell into hands of the enemy.

could argue that it should never have seceded from the state as established by David; and, anyway, Judah had not fallen then. Jerusalem had been inviolate, protected by the Lord, and there was a rock-like confidence that so it would remain. Yet now Jerusalem was in ruins, and they were in exile. Could this mean that God had washed His hands of the Jewish people? That their association had ended?

Torn by such doubt, the nation might have gone under. Bereft of faith in the Lord who had stopped listening, the exiles might have turned to the religion of the region and adapted themselves to Babylonian customs, practices and patterns of thought. Withtin two or three generations they might have become assimilated into the predominante society, as did all the other conquered and exiled peoples who are today just names in history books. They would have become indistinguishable in the human landscape. They would no longer have been Jews. What helped to save them were the words of the prophets.

The exiles, after all, were a sophisticated group. As the Bible indicates, those deported to Babylon were priests, technicians, professionals and intellectuals. They were thinking men, and as they struggled over this dark problem of destiny, recalling again and again the now treasured words of their seers, they began to see glimmerings of light. The prophets had grappled with this very problem, meeting it in advance of events, and this was particularly evident in Jeremiah, Ezekiel and Habakkuk. They had concluded that if catastrophe came, it would be the product not of divine indifference but of divine justice, and that a change of behavior in Hebrew society would bring a change of fortune. They had sought desperately to uproot popular illusion and false hope precisely in order to sow the seed of authentic hope. In urging the people to repent of their iniquities they had stressed the warning that punishment, if they failed to do so, would even extend to the loss of Jerusalem and their land. *But this did not mean that they had been abandoned by God.* If they continued to keep the faith and live a just and ethical life, the nation would be preserved and would return to its land.

Thus, from the tragic heart of Jeremiah,

We... charge ourselves yearly with the third part of a shekel for the service of the house of our God (Nehemiah 10:32)

Handle of a jar stamped with the letters "Yrslm" (left), Hebrew for Jerusalem. Such jars bearing the name of the holy city are believed to have been used for contributions to the Temple.
An ancient coin found in Israel bearing the name "Yahud" (right) in early Hebrew script. Yahud was the official name of the province of Judah during the Persian period.

these words come bursting through, and they made a profound impact upon the exiles particularly because they were uttered by the man who had not indulged in false encouragement but had realistically prophesied destruction: "Then fear not, O Jacob my servant, says the Lord, nor be dismayed, O Israel; for lo, I will save you from afar, and your offspring from the land of their captivity . . . I will make a full end of all the nations among whom I scattered you, but of you I will not make a full end . . . Behold, I will restore the fortunes of the tents of Jacob, and have compassion on his dwellings; the city shall be rebuilt upon its mound, and the palace shall stand where it used to be" (Jer. 30:10, 11, 18). The nation had suffered heavy punishment, but, said Jeremiah: "Thus says the Lord: . . . I have loved you with an everlasting love; therefore I have continued my faithfulness to you. Again I will build you, and you shall be built, O virgin Israel! . . . he who scattered Israel will gather him, and will keep him as a shepherd keeps his flock. For the Lord has ransomed Jacob, and has redeemed him from hands too strong for him. They

He who scattered Israel will gather him, and will keep him as a shepherd keeps his flock

(Jeremiah 31:10)

Jeremiah sought to console his people exiled to Babylon with the prophecy that the Lord would shepherd and gather up his scattered flock and bring them back to their own land.

shall come and sing aloud on the height of Zion, and they shall be radiant over the goodness of the Lord, over the grain, the wine, and the oil, and over the young of the flock and the herd; their life shall be like a watered garden, and they shall languish no more. Then shall the maidens rejoice in the dance, and the young men and the old shall be merry. I will turn their mourning into joy, I will comfort them, and give them gladness for sorrow . . . and they shall come back from the land of the enemy. There is hope for your future, says the Lord, and your children shall come back to their own country" (Jer. 31:3–4, 10–13, 16–17).

Habakkuk offered a similar message of hope, and the exiles in Babylon could identify with him for he had been as perplexed as they. He saw evil all around him, "destruction and violence . . . strife and contention . . . [and] justice goes forth perverted" (Hab. 1:3, 4), and in a visionary dialogue with God, he wondered at what seemed to be the Lord's indifference. Then, speaking just after the Babylonians had inflicted their decisive de-

Write the vision, make it plain upon tablets (Habakkuk 2:2)

Folios from the Commentary on the Book of Habakkuk, the prophet who gave hope to the exiles. They are part of a complete Dead Sea Scroll discovered in the caves of Qumran and now on display in Jerusalem.

feat on the Egyptians at Carchemish (in 605), with Nebuchadnezzar emerging as the new master of the Middle East, he foresaw the coming invasion of Judah. He knew that the Babylonians were being used as an instrument of "chastisement", but he was still troubled that God was "silent when the wicked swallows up the man more righteous than he" (Hab. 1:12, 13). God told the prophet to "Write the vision; make it plain upon tablets, so he may run who reads it". The answer would come, but not yet, "For still the vision awaits its time . . . If it seem slow, wait for it". But "it will surely come", and then "he whose soul is not upright in him shall fail, but the righteous shall live by his faith" (Hab. 2:2–4).

Because the exiles could understand his bewilderment, they could also, in their bereaved plight, find strength in Habakkuk's final affirmation: "Though the fig tree do not blossom, nor fruit be on the vines, the produce of the olive fail and the fields yield no food, the flock be cut off from the fold and there be no herd in the stalls, yet I will rejoice in the Lord, I will joy in the God of my salvation. God, the Lord, is my strength; He makes my feet like hinds' feet, he makes me tread upon my high places" (Hab. 3:17–19).

THE PROMISE OF EZEKIEL

The exiles, victims of imperial might, who could see all around them the manifold features of arrogant power, might have been cowed into a sense of futility. Could such might indeed be brought low? The prophets' predictions of the fall of empires could give them comfort and genuine hope; for these, after all, were the very prophets who had foreseen the fall of Judah, and had had the courage to say so, and they were certainly not given to specious promises. Thus, their people, who were now in exile, could take heart from their more sanguine utterances. They now recalled that Zephaniah had said that the lands of the enemy would be "possessed by nettles and salt pits, and a waste for ever" (2:9). And the gloomy Jeremiah had made a direct prediction of the fall of Babylon: "I will requite Babylon and all the inhabitants of Chaldea before your very eyes for all the evil that they have done in Zion, says the Lord . . . and Babylon shall become

and Babylon shall become a heap of ruins, the haunt of jackals, a horror and a hissing, without inhabitant (Jeremiah 51:37)

The ruins of Babylon. 48 years after the Babylonians had sacked Jerusalem and exiled its survivors, they were themselves vanquished by the Persians, and the Jews were allowed to return to their homeland.

a heap of ruins, the haunt of jackals, a horror and a hissing, without inhabitant" (Jer. 51:24, 37). Ezekiel, too, had invisioned the destruction of all who had ever harmed Israel, suiting his metaphor to the principal characteristic of each enemy: Of Egypt, "the great dragon" of the Nile, the Lord "will put hooks in your jaws" (Ez. 29:3, 4). Of mercantile Tyre with its vast fleets: "Your riches, your wares, your merchandise, your mariners and your pilots, your caulkers . . . and all your men of war who are in you, with all your company that is in your midst, [will] sink into the heart of the seas on the day of your ruin" (27:27).

The prophet Nahum confined himself exclusively to this theme. He was addressing himself to the fate of Nineveh, that "bloody city, all full of lies and booty" (3:1), capital of the great Assyrian empire, and he was predicting (or describing) its downfall (in 612). To the Jewish exiles only a few decades later — as to those in later centuries — his powerful and vivid depiction had an urgent topical appeal, symbolic of what could, and would, happen to all who oppressed Israel.

An avenging army was descending upon Nineveh: "The shield of his mighty men is red, his soldiers are clothed in scarlet. The chariots rage in the streets, they rush to and fro through the squares; they gleam like torches, they dart like lightning . . . The crack of whip, the rumble of wheel, galloping horse and bounding chariot! Horsemen charging, flashing sword and glittering spear, hosts of slain, heaps of corpses, dead bodies without end" (Nahum 2:3, 4; 3:2, 3). "Halt! Halt!", cry the people of the capital, but "Nineveh is like a pool whose waters run away" (2:8). Nahum's magic words brought to life the very scenes which the unhappy exiles had witnessed — when they themselves had been the victims. It was comforting to feel that the fate of the mighty Assyrians could equally overtake the Babylonian empire (as indeed it did, not long afterwards).

[Incidentally, among the Dead Sea scrolls found in the caves of Qumran were portions of two Commentaries, one on the Book of Habakkuk and the other on the Book of Nahum. Both were written in the 1st century

O dry bones... Behold, I will cause breath to enter you, and you shall live... O my people; and I will bring you home into the land of Israel (Ezekiel 37: 4, 5, 12)

The prophet Ezekiel's vision of the Valley of Dry Bones and the promise of the Jewish return from exile to their homeland, as portrayed in successive sequences in the biblical wall paintings of the ancient synagogue of Dura-Europos.

BC and the "fall of empire" theme was again given a contemporary context.]

All this was reassuring to the exiles, for it showed the feasibility of their hope of freedom. As to the likelihood of its realization, the promise in the words of Ezekiel was as sustaining as the hopefulness of Jeremiah, for his warnings of doom had been equally pitiless. (As a youth in Jerusalem, Ezekiel may well have heard some of the tirades of Jeremiah.) Moreover, as one of the first to taste the gall of exile, having been deported as a Temple priest together with king Jehoiachin in 597, he was closer both in the flesh and the spirit to the later exiles. He was a strange figure, mystical and ecstatic, given to bizarre symbols and strange mimes, and the exiles could recall the occasion, before the fall of Jerusalem, when, to give dramatic impact to his warning, he had "acted out" the siege of the city. He marked out a diagram of Jerusalem on a clay tablet, with a representation of siege-works around it. He lay beside it, and each day he would eat a minute ration of food, and drink sparingly of water, to indicate what conditions would be like. Final-

ly he cut his hair and beard and flung a third in the midst of the diagram and burnt it, to symbolize those who would be slain inside the city; spread another third with a sword outside the city for those who would be killed beyond the walls; and scattered the last third to signify the deportations (Ez. 4, 5). On another occasion, he mimed the act of exile by making a hole in the wall of his house and emerging from it carrying "an exile's baggage" (12:3).

This grotesque but prescient representation of tragedy lent greater force to his words of hope when he did find himself moved to utter them. This is believed to have occurred when he was already in exile and had been joined by the later deportees, and they drew great encouragement from his: "Thus says the Lord God ... you, O mountains of Israel, shall shoot forth your branches, and yield your fruit to my people Israel; for they will soon come home ... and you shall be tilled and sown; and I will multiply men upon you, the whole house of Israel, all of it; the cities shall be inhabited and the waste places re-

On the willows there we hung up our lyres *(Psalms 137:2)*

Ancient lyres (left) depicted in Assyrian reliefs discovered in Babylon,
and the willow tree (right) in today's Israel. Their captors called
for a song from the Jewish exiles in Babylon, but the Jews put away
their lyres, vowing never to sing until they were restored to their own land.

built; and I will multiply upon you man and beast; and they shall increase and be fruitful . . ." (Ez. 36:7–11). They were greatly moved — as their descendants would be throughout their centuries of exile — by the celebrated Ezekiel vision of the valley of dry bones and the promise of the Return. Set down by the "hand of the Lord" in the midst of the valley and moved by "the Spirit of the Lord" to "Prophesy to these bones, and say to them . . . Behold, I will cause breath to enter you, and you shall live", Ezekiel "prophesied as I was commanded". And as he prophesied, "there was a noise, and behold, a rattling; and the bones came together, bone to its bone. And as I looked, there were sinews on them, and flesh had come upon them, and skin had covered them . . . and the breath came into them, and they lived, and stood upon their feet, an exceedingly great host. Then he said to me, 'Son of man, these bones are the whole house of Israel. Behold, they say, Our bones are dried up, and our hope is lost; we are clean cut off. Therefore prophesy, and say to them, Thus says the Lord God: . . . O my people . . . I will bring you home into the land of Israel . . . And I will put my Spirit within you, and you shall live; and I will place you in your own land . . ." (Ez. 37:1–14).

"IF I FORGET YOU, O JERUSALEM"
Armed with their sacred writings and lifted up by the powerful words of the prophets, the Israelites in Babylonian exile could come to terms with their fate by remaining true to their faith and harboring hope. The Lord was with them even in exile. They accordingly shut themselves off from the practices of the people around them and followed their own unique customs, observing the *Shabbat* and the rite of circumcision. They retained their own worship. With no Temple, they established prayer halls (synagogues), and substituted prayer for sacrifice. They pored over the sacred Books of Moses and the utterances of the earlier prophets, absorbing the wonders and the tragedies of their dramatic history and seeking encouragement in every word. In their hearts they carried the living memory of Jerusalem and Judah, and they vowed never to forget:

"By the waters of Babylon,
there we sat down and wept,
when we remembered Zion" — and their
haunting cry echoed down all the centuries
of Jewish history.
"On the willows there we hung up our lyres.
For there our captors required of us songs,
and our tormentors, mirth, saying, 'Sing us
one of the songs of Zion!'
How shall we sing the Lord's song in a
foreign land?
If I forget you, O Jerusalem, let my right
hand wither!
Let my tongue cleave to the roof of my mouth,
if I do not remember you,
if I do not set Jerusalem above my highest
joy!" (Psalm 137)

The exiles in Babylon remembered. Thus
did they preserve their national and religious
identity.

One particular group of prophetic utterances served as a special aid to remembrance,
giving almost tangible form to their faith in
the restoration of Jerusalem and Judah. This
was a kind of blueprint in which the prophet
Ezekiel laid down provisions for the restored
Israelite State of the future (Ez. 40-48).
Part of his national and religious system in
the renewed state, such as the form of administration and the tribal locations, were
utopian and idealized. But integral to Ezekiel's vision was the restoration of Jerusalem
as the centre of the nation, with a rebuilt
Temple and prescribed regulations for Temple
worship; and his description, particularly of
the Temple, was as meticulously detailed as
an architect's drawing, complete with every
conceivable measurement of each room, door,
window, wall and gate. Ezekiel, as we have
seen, had been a Temple priest in his younger
years, and he was clearly drawing on a photo-
graphic memory. His words gave an exact
shape to the dream of the exiles, and of their
children born in exile, and greater force to
their will to fulfil it.

[It was Ezekiel's description of the Temple
gates which confirmed this century's discoveries by archaeologists, notably Yigael Yadin,
of the gates to three of the cities which had
been constructed by king Solomon, "Hazor
and Megiddo and Gezer" (I Kings 9:15).
Excavations at all three sites yielded identical

And behold, there was a wall all around the outside of the temple area (Ezekiel 40:5)

Jews throughout Israel and Jewish pilgrims the world over throng to the Western Wall in Jerusalem on the Ninth day of the Hebrew month of Av, the day of mourning for the destruction of the Temple.

city gates at the 10th century level. Each had a tower on either side of the entrance, and the gatehouse for the guards consisted of six chambers, three on each side. This matched perfectly the eloquent detailing of the eastern wall of the Temple in the vision of Ezekiel: "Then he went into the gateway facing east, going up its steps, and measured the threshold of the gate, one reed deep . . . Then he measured the vestibule of the gateway, eight cubits . . . And there were three side rooms on either side of the east gate; the three were of the same size . . ." (Ez. 40:6–10). Since the prophet was familiar with the Temple, he was clearly describing in his vision a gate which he had actually seen — and whose measurements he could recapitulate — and this eastern gate of the Temple had assuredly been designed by the same Solomonic architect who had been responsible for the construction of the gates at Hazor, Gezer and Megiddo.]

THE RESTORATION
While dreaming and yearning, the exiles in Babylon also followed events in the region

Jerusalem at the time of the Second Temple,
a scale model reconstruction by Professor
Michael Avi-Yonah in the garden of
the Holyland Hotel, Jerusalem.

with the closest interest, ever on the lookout for signs of change in the fortunes of the imperial contestants which might signal their redemption. Change was on the way with the sudden rise of Cyrus, who, sooner than anyone — apart from the prophets — could have imagined, would vanquish the Babylonians and found a new Persian empire. Those scholars who consider that the last 26 chapters of the Book of Isaiah were written by "the Second Isaiah" place his ministry in Babylon during this period of impending change. The traditionalists, who hold to a single 8th/7th century Isaiah and consider that his was a vision of the future, also regard his prophecy as relating to these Babylonian times. But whichever Isaiah it was, both schools agree that his words in these late chapters exerted a powerful influence on the exiles, strengthening their morale and bolstering their hope. The prophet did even more for the future generations of Jews — and civilization in general — for though his immediate concern was the Jewish fate, his profound thought and sublime expression had a universal and timeless appeal. God was all powerful, master

of creation and of all subsequent development. His aim was the just society, and in the achievement of this ideal, there was a special role for the descendants of Abraham. The people of Israel were to be "a light to the nations, to open the eyes that are blind, to bring out the prisoners from the dungeon" (Isa. 42:6, 7). Israel had sinned, and was punished, and Babylon had been used as the divine rod. Now Israel was to be restored, and Cyrus would be used as the divine instrument of retribution against Babylon and of compassion towards Israel. "Cyrus . . . shall fulfil all my purpose; saying of Jerusalem, 'She shall be built', and of the temple, 'Your foundation shall be laid'" (Isa. 44:28).

To those who thought, in this age of great empires, that the source of their might lay with their imperial deities, the prophet elaborated on the Mosaic commandments, scorning the very idea that events could be determined by blocks of wood or stone, and presenting monotheism in its clearest form. "Who has measured the waters in the hollow of his hand and marked off the heavens with a span, enclosed the dust of the earth in a measure and weighed the mountains in scales and the hills in a balance?... Behold, the nations are like a drop from a bucket, and are accounted as the dust on the scales; behold, he takes up the isles like fine dust... Who has directed the Spirit of the Lord... Whom did he consult for his enlightenment...?" Was it these man-made inanimate objects "who taught him the path of justice, and taught him knowledge, and showed him the way of understanding?" (Isa. 40:12–15). The prophet was speaking in a pagan world, and with homely parable and withering irony he fashioned a courageous statement demolishing idolatry which has remained a classic to this day. "To whom then will you liken God...? The idol! a work-man casts it... All who make idols are nothing, and the things they delight in do not profit... Who fashions a god or casts an image, that is profitable for nothing?... The ironsmith fashions it and works it over the coals; he shapes it with hammers, and forges it with his strong arm; he becomes hungry and his strength fails, he drinks no water and is faint. The carpenter... fashions it with planes, and...

shapes it into the figure of a man ... he plants a cedar and the rain nourishes it. Then it becomes fuel for a man; he takes a part of it and warms himself, he kindles a fire and bakes bread; also he makes a god and worships it, he makes it a graven image and falls down before it. Half of it he burns in the fire; over the half he eats flesh, he roasts meat and is satisfied; also he warms himself and says, 'Aha, I am warm, I have seen the fire!' And the rest of it he makes into a god, his idol; and falls down to it and worships it; he prays to it and says, 'Deliver me, for thou art my god!'" (Isa. 40:18, 19 and 44:9–17).

Through such prophetic utterances, the Jews in Babylon adhered to the Hebrew way of life, spurning the pagan ways of their host country, believing more than ever that exile was only temporary, and clinging to the conviction that they would return to their homeland.

Fulfilment was not long delayed. Less than fifty years after it had overrun Judah and gained dominion over the entire region, the great Babylonian empire collapsed, overwhelmed by Cyrus. By the year 538, Baby-

he plants a cedar... Then it becomes fuel for a man; he takes a part of it and warms himself, he kindles a fire and bakes bread... And the rest of it he makes into a god, his idol; and falls down to it and worships it (Isaiah 44:14, 15, 17)

Scorning the pagans who fashioned images
and then called them gods to whom they bowed
in worship, the prophet Isaiah used
homely parable and withering irony to make
his timeless statement against idolatry.

lon's imperial territories, including the former kingdom of Judah, had come under Persian control.

Cyrus was one of the rare rulers of his times, wise, enlightened and tolerant. Where others had brutalized their subjects and sought to terrorize them into conformity with the customs of the reigning regime, Cyrus offered cultural and religious autonomy to his heterogeneous vanquished subjects — and often entrusted the administration to one of their own leaders. In the first year of his reign, he issued a decree which was to have a momentous impact on Jewish history: he proclaimed himself in favor of the restoration of the Jewish community in their own land. They could rebuild their Temple in Jerusalem and his royal treasury would contribute towards the expenses. The holy vessels removed by Nebuchadnezzar would be restored. Jews who remained in Babylon would be encouraged to aid the returnees and offer financial support for the reconstruction of their central sanctuary. Placed in charge of this "Return to Zion" movement was "Sheshbazzar, the prince of Judah", and he was appointed Gov-

ernor of Judah. Sheshbazzar applied himself immediately to the task of building the new Temple on the site of the old. How much was done by him and how much under his successor is not known, for the biblical report telescopes the accounts of Sheshbazzar and his nephew, Zerubbabel, who followed him as Governor, crediting most of the work to the latter.

It is evident, however, that progress in the ruined city was very slow. The task of reconstruction was gigantic, yet the sparse population of returnees were harassed by poverty (the early years were marked by successive crop failures), by raids from neighboring enemies, and by political obstruction from Persian officials in adjoining Samaria. By the time Cyrus died, killed during one of his campaigns in 530, little more than the foundations of the Second Temple had been laid. Not much more had been accomplished by the year 522 when his son and successor, Cambyses, took his life. It was only when the third Persian monarch, the formidable Darius I, ascended the throne that work was renewed in earnest, and seven years later, in

Thus says Cyrus king of Persia... Whoever is among you of all his the house of the Lord, the God of Israel *(Ezra 1:2, 3)*

The tomb of Cyrus the Great (right), founder of the
Persian empire, at Pasargadae, the royal city which
he built, and which was supplanted some years later by
Persepolis (left), 30 miles to the southwest, where Darius the
Great founded a new royal residence. Cyrus overthrew the
Babylonians and allowed and aided the Jewish exiles to return
to their homeland. Darius continued Cyrus' policy.

515, the Temple was completed. "And the
people of Israel, the priests and the Levites,
and the rest of the returned exiles, celebrated
the dedication of this house of God with joy"
(Ezra 6:16).

Darius had introduced greater stability and
order in the region, had renewed the promise
of Cyrus to Judah and given encouragement
to the restoration project for Jerusalem.
But among the leading spirits rousing the returnees to apply themselves with all intensity
to living the just life and reviving their central
sanctuary were Haggai and Zechariah. (They,
together with Malachi, who belonged to the
next generation, are traditionally considered
to have been "the last of the prophets".)
They shared the hardships of their fellow
pioneers, the early returnees to Judah from
Babylon; but they were neither depressed by
the misfortunes of the initial years nor cowed
by the immensity of the restoration goal. Their
rallying words, like those of their predecessors, were compounded of rebuke, exhorta-
tion to righteousness, and hope. Haggai was
aghast at the lethargy which seemed to have
overtaken his people who had set out from

Babylon with such high ideals, yet who now appeared to be taken with building their own private dwellings rather than the House of the Lord, with improving their material lot instead of advancing the welfare of the nation. No wonder they had suffered harassment and blight. It was "Because of my house that lies in ruins, while you busy yourselves each with his own house". He told them to "Go up to the hills and bring wood and build the house [of God]" (Hag. 1:8, 9). And they did.

Zechariah's visions were more mystical and symbolic, but, like Haggai, he also saw the re-established Temple as the focal centre of the people's faith and the vital core of a revived national community. He was equally concerned with social justice and fairness in human relations. "Render true judgements, show kindness and mercy each to his brother, do not oppress the widow, the fatherless, the sojourner, or the poor; and let none of you devise evil against his brother in your heart" (Zech. 7:9, 10). Amidst the political turmoil in the Persian empire between the death of Cyrus and the accession of Darius, the two prophets were also seized by the prospect of a completely liberated Judah, and they expressed the messianic hope for a restored and purified Jewish kingdom. The Lord, prophesied Haggai, was "about to shake the heavens and the earth, and to overthrow the throne of kingdoms" (Hag. 2:21, 22). With the empires destroyed, and Judah no longer in subjection, the Lord "will return to Zion", says Zechariah, "and will dwell in the midst of Jerusalem, and Jerusalem shall be called the faithful city, and the mountain of the Lord of hosts, the holy mountain" (Zech. 8:3). Zechariah then describes the color and mood of the restored and untroubled city, no longer afflicted by wars and expulsions, where people would live in tranquility to a ripe age, and welcome their brothers from exile. "Old men and old women shall again sit in the streets of Jerusalem, each with staff in hand for very age. And . . . the city shall be full of boys and girls playing in its streets". It would be "marvellous in the sight of the remnant of this people in these days . . . says the Lord of hosts: Behold, I will save my people from the east country and from the west country; and I will bring them to dwell in

Jerusalem and part of Judah, as they appear
in the 6th century mosaic map discovered at
Madeba, in Jordan, southeast of the Dead Sea.

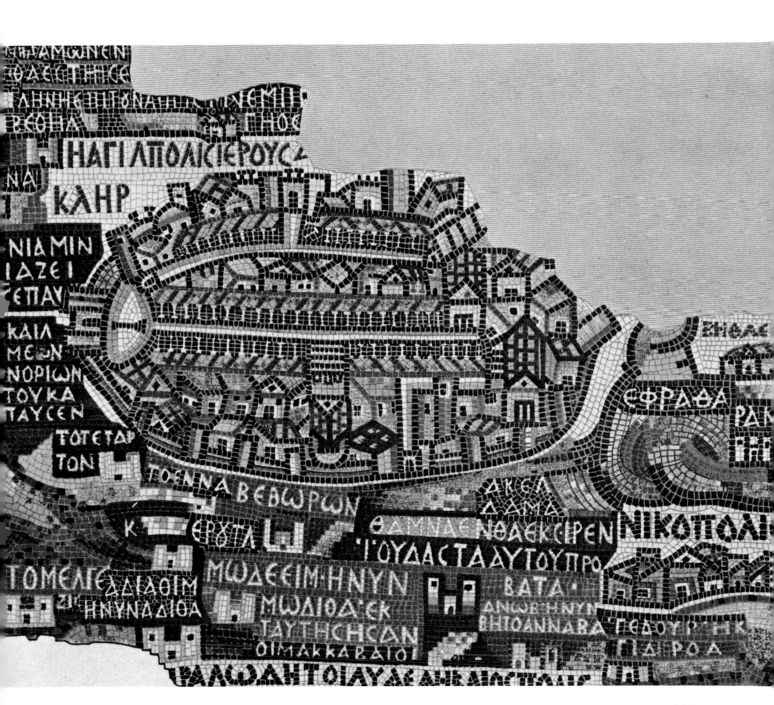

The rose-red rock of Petra, located in the land of the Edomites who were so fiercely denounced by the prophet Obadiah for aiding the enemies of Israel, exulting in her humiliation and taking advantage of her reverses.

the midst of Jerusalem; and they shall be my people and I will be their God, in faithfulness and in righteousness" (Zech. 8:4–8).

Malachi, who prophesied at the very end of the 6th century BC (though some scholars put him half a century later), found that even though the Temple had now been rebuilt, there was religious laxity and a lowering of moral standards, and he took both priesthood and public to task. (His words, in particular, would influence Nehemiah and Ezra to introduce their religious reforms.) Their wrongdoing was an "abomination", a profanation of "the sanctuary of the Lord" and of "the covenant of our fathers" (Mal. 2:10, 11). There is a stern echo of Zechariah's appeal for just behavior: "I will be a swift witness against the sorcerers, against the adulterers, against those who swear falsely, against those who oppress the hireling in his wages, the widow and the orphan . . . says the Lord" (Mal. 3:5). And he, too, continuing the powerful thread of the Covenant tradition, ends his utterance with this reminder from the Lord: "Remember the law of my servant Moses, the statutes and ordinances that I commanded him at Horeb [Sinai] for all Israel" (Mal. 4:4).

The full independence sought by the wave of Jewish returnees from exile to Judah in the latter part of the 6th century BC was slow to arrive; but what they established, through the inspired words of the prophets, was a firm enough base upon which their successors in the 5th century, those who returned under Nehemiah and Ezra, could build a community in their own land with a specific and enduring national and religious identity.

There is obscurity about the dates of the three remaining Minor Prophets, Jonah, Joel and Obadiah, for there is no specific reference in their Books, as there is in the works of the other prophets, linking them to the reign of a particular king or to an event mentioned elsewhere in the Bible whose period is known. Some commentators hold to the traditional view that they prophesied as early as the 8th century BC; others consider that Joel and Obadiah belonged to the 5th and Jonah to as late as the 3rd century BC.

The Book of Jonah is popularly known for its story of the "whale" and for the fact that

> *And the Lord God appointed a plant, and made it come up over Jonah, that it might be a shade over his head* (Jonah 4:6)

it contains only a single line of prophecy: "Yet forty days, and Nineveh shall be overthrown!" (Jonah 3:4) — and even that prediction is not fulfilled. Yet whatever its date and historical context, its fundamental instructional themes set in fascinating narrative make clear why it was included in the canonical collection of the twelve short prophetic Books. It is basically a dramatic message of divine compassion.

The reluctant Jonah takes flight in the opposite direction when he is ordered by God to hasten to Nineveh and upbraid its people for their wickedness. But a prophet cannot evade his divine assignment, and the Lord harnesses the elements to bring him back — inside the belly of a "great fish". He proceeds to Nineveh and utters his warning of imminent destruction, whereupon the people, from the king down, promptly repent. They fast, don sack-cloth and sit in ashes, and the Lord renounces punishment and spares them.

Jonah is furious, insisting that they must pay for their sins. He then reveals that he had fled from his mission precisely because he suspected this is what might happen; for

The castor plant, which figured in the parable of Jonah, springing up overnight to give the prophet shade, but soon withering, leaving him without shelter from the scorching sun.

"I knew that thou art a gracious God and merciful, slow to anger, and abounding in steadfast love, and repentest of evil" (Jonah 4:2). But he still cannot believe that Nineveh will escape retribution, and he goes outside the city to wait and see. God then causes a castor-plant to spring up overnight to give him shade, but sends a worm next morning to attack it. The plant withers, and Jonah suffers all the ills from a scorching sun and a sultry east wind without shelter. Then God asks him whether he is "angry for the plant". "I do well to be angry", says Jonah, "angry enough to die". "You pity the plant", says God, "for which you did not labour, nor did you make it grow, which came into being in a night, and perished in a night. And should not I pity Nineveh...?" (Jonah 4:9–11).

The Book of Obadiah, the shortest in the Bible (consisting of only one chapter), is a fierce denunciation of Edom for aiding the enemies of Israel, exulting in her humiliation and taking advantage of her reverses. Edom had occupied parts of Judah, had "gloated over his [Judah's] disaster... looted his goods in the day of his calamity... cut off his fugitives... [and] delivered up his survivors in the day of distress" (Obad. 1:13, 14).

Obadiah predicted that Edom and all the nations who wronged Israel would be brought low: "You who live in the clefts of the rock, whose dwelling is high, who say in your heart, 'Who will bring me down to the ground?' Though you soar aloft like the eagle, though your nest is set among the stars, thence will I bring you down, says the Lord" (Obad. 1:3, 4). The independence and the territories of Israel would be restored, "saviours shall go up to Mount Zion... and the kingdom shall be the Lord's" (Obad. 1:21).

Joel was an apocalyptic prophet who used language of great power and beauty to set down his vision of the imminence of divine judgement. It would be heralded by devastation, and the metaphor he used was the ravage committed by a swarm of locusts. It is perhaps the most vivid, precise and poetic description of this phenomenon ever composed. Following this judgement, and the punishment of all who had oppressed Israel, a new world of purity would arise, with Jerusalem

220

as its jewel. Judah would become a land of fruitfulness whose "mountains shall drip sweet wine, and the hills shall flow with milk, and all the stream beds ... shall flow with water; and a fountain shall come forth from the house of the Lord ... [and] Judah shall be inhabited for ever, and Jerusalem to all generations ... for the Lord dwells in Zion" (Joel 3:18-21). He called upon his people to prepare for this coming Day of the Lord "in the valley of decision" by true penitence and a return to righteous ways, the righteousness of conscience and of behavior. "Rend your hearts", he told them "not your garments" (Joel 2:13).

These, then, were the men who founded and developed the Jewish nation and its religion, fashioned a supreme body of ethics which has influenced almost half the human race, and established ideals which still remain the aspiration of civilized society. First, through the bleak desert of Sinai, and later, amid the rugged landscape of Israel, in war and peace, in times of anarchy and in times of order, of turbulence and quiescence, of splendor and squalor, these spiritual giants of old strode with firm tread and fearless heart, uttering words of timeless wisdom which thundered down the ages to change the life and behavior of man.

Their visionary pronouncements expressed in sublime language were intended for the ears of their own generations of Jews, yet they became the "portable homeland" of the Jewish people throughout their centuries of exile — and led to the rebirth of the State of Israel in our own day. They were aimed at their own nation, yet they became universal and eternal, and are today the heritage of all western nations. The prophets sought to influence contemporary events, and did not always succeed. Instead, they changed the course of history.

Jerusalem, built as a city which is bound firmly together... Pray for the peace of Jerusalem!... Peace be within you

(Psalms 122:3, 6, 8)

AMASIA
Capadocia

ARMENIA

Cori-
Beleania
Soltanea
Analiba
Iassus
Dagusa
Anzeta
Das Grosse
AR MENIA

Metilena
Semisus
Iuliopolis
Arsamesata

Camana
Sisoatra

MINOR
Samosa
ta
Taurus geburg
Saccana
Dor

LICONIA
Leandis
Entelia
Taurus Geburg
Vrina
Porsica
Suma
Nisibis

Flaviopolis
Badinum
Edessa
Ombrea
Das Geburg Mescha
Sinna

ASIA
Diocesaria
Irinopolis
Cesaria
Nicopolis
Antiochia
Singa
Zeugma
Balatha
Haran
MESO

CILICIA
Celeucia
Latmos
Soli
MINOR
Calamana
Regia
Mergob
PADDAN
ARAM
Zan

Celenaris
Tarsur
Adena
Isus
COMAGENA
Deba
Caonia
Beroca
Acraba
Schweer Vatter Flu[ss]

Zephirium
Baca
Amanus Mons
Sibres
Bene
Zura
Elia
PO

MEER
Chdes
Iny
Alexandria
M Pieria
Chalcis
Alalis
Alamatha
Maube
Chabora
TAM

Olimphus P
Golgi
Dinare
tum
Das Ißische Meer
Antiochia
Calibon
Tipsacus
Thelda

Afradisium
Salamis
Das Selzu[m]
SYRIA
Asachi
Apamia
nun Alep
Orisa
Adada
Euphra[t]

USN
Litu
um
Grega
Surische
Meer
Laodicea
Seleucus
ARAM
Putea
Dadara

Martium
Curias Pr
Orthosia
Prexon
Epiphania
Emessa
Palmira mi
Danabarena
Dedan
Balagala
Cathan

DISCHE MEER
oßen Meers
Tripolis
Gabila
Larasa
Phoeni
cien
M Hermon
Averia
Se heba
Sabe

Adonis fluh
Heliopolis
Iabruda
Cagana
Kadar.
Rega

Ionas flihet vor dem
Herren Ion.J v.3
Sidon
Tirus
Das
Damascus
Land Huss
Pharphar
Gera
Der weg so Iacob
Eleme
Choce
Saccea
Alata
DAS

MEER Iaphe oder Ioppe
von welchem
Ionas abgefahren
Ptolomais
Cesaria
Capernaum
Lida
Sichem
Cananiten
Keneriten
TRACO
NITEN
Land
Adra
Rabba
Bostra
Nabathea
oder Hebreisch
Nabaioth
Agreni
CUS

Heviten
Pheresiten
Ierusalem
AMO
RITEN
Cademoth
Suriata
Erupa
W

Ascalon
Iebusiten
Amoriten
Kenuten
Cades
Das Land
Seir
Trana
Necla
Adron
Steinicht
Arabien
Zizi
Rablath
ISMAELITEN
Thauba
Seraa
Naph

Pelusium
Phaan
Die
WusteZin
oder
Cades
EDOMI
TEN
Ame
le
Auta
Moca
Obera
Aguben
ARA
ISMA
Banacha

Cairus
Sinat
Herck
Mara
Zur
Das Land
MADI
Aramana
Ostama
Das Reich
ARABIEN
Das ist das Reich
Das
Arabische

Elath
AN.
Ancale